RACHEL CARSON AND ECOLOGY FOR KIDS

FOR KIDS

HER LIFE AND IDEAS, WITH 21
ACTIVITIES AND EXPERIMENTS

ROWENA RAE

CHICAGO
REVIEW
PRESS

Published by Chicago Review Press, Incorporated
814 North Franklin Street
Chicago, Illinois 60610
ISBN 978-0-89733-933-9

Library of Congress Cataloging-in-Publication Data
Names: Rae, Rowena, author.
Title: Rachel Carson and ecology for kids : her life and ideas, with 21
  activities and experiments / Rowena Rae.
Description: Chicago, Illinois : Chicago Review Press, [2020] | Includes
  bibliographical references and index. | Audience: Ages 9 to 12 |
  Audience: Grades 4–6 | Summary: "Rachel Carson and Ecology for Kids
  explores the life and ideas of American biologist, conservationist, and
  science writer Rachel Carson, who served as the catalyst of the modern
  environmental movement"—Provided by publisher.
Identifiers: LCCN 2019035062 (print) | LCCN 2019035063 (ebook) |
  ISBN 9780897339339 (trade paperback) | ISBN 9780897339346 (pdf) |
  ISBN 9780897339353 (mobi) | ISBN 9780897339360 (epub)
Subjects: LCSH: Carson, Rachel, 1907–1964—Juvenile literature. |
  Biologists—United States—Biography—Juvenile literature. |
  Environmentalists—United States—Biography—Juvenile literature.
Classification: LCC QH31.C33 R334 2020 (print) | LCC QH31.C33
  (ebook) | DDC 570.92 [B]—dc23
LC record available at https://lccn.loc.gov/2019035062
LC ebook record available at https://lccn.loc.gov/2019035063

Cover and interior design: Sarah Olson
Cover images: (front cover) Monarch butterfly, iStock.com/XKarDoc;
Carson's Cat, Beinecke Rare Book and Manuscript Library, Yale
University; Bald eagle, iStock.com/BrianEKushner; Rachel Carson and
Bob Hines, Rex Gary Schmidt/by permission of Rachel Carson Council,
Inc.; Milkweed, iStock.com/chas53; Carson with binoculars, Shirley A.
Briggs/by permission of Rachel Carson Council, Inc.; Rachel Carson
National Wildlife Refuge, Wikimedia Commons/Captain-tucker;
(back cover) Sanderling, istock.com/BrianLasenby; Carson examining
a sea star, by permission of Rachel Carson Council, Inc.; Button,
Smithsonian National Museum of American History; The shore in front
of Carson's cottage, Rowena Rae; Oysters, Shutterstock/zcw; Great blue
heron, Shutterstock/Susan Rydberg
Interior illustrations: Rowena Rae and Jim Spence

Printed in the United States of America
5 4 3 2 1

For my parents, Ann and Angus,
and for my daughters,
Genevieve and Madeleine.

CONTENTS

TIME LINE

1907 May 27, Rachel Carson is born in Springdale, Pennsylvania

1918 Carson's first published story is printed in *St. Nicholas* magazine

1925 Carson graduates top of her high school class

1929 Carson graduates *magna cum laude* with a biology degree from Pennsylvania College for Women

Carson sees the ocean for the first time in her life

1932 Carson earns a master of science degree from Johns Hopkins University

1934 Carson abandons her doctoral work to get a full-time job

1935 Robert Carson, Rachel's father, dies

1936 Carson is hired by the Bureau of Fisheries as a junior aquatic biologist

1937 Marian Carson Williams, Rachel's sister, dies. Rachel and her mother take over the care of Marian's daughters, Virginia, 12, and Marjorie, 11

Carson's article "Undersea" is published in the *Atlantic Monthly*

1939 Paul Müller discovers that a synthesized chemical called DDT kills insects. DDT becomes the first widely used synthetic insecticide

1941 Carson's first book, *Under the Sea-Wind*, is published by Simon & Schuster

1951 Carson's second book, *The Sea Around Us*, is published by Oxford University Press and becomes a bestseller

1952 Carson resigns from the Fish and Wildlife Service (formerly Bureau of Fisheries)

Carson receives many awards including the National Book Award for Nonfiction and the John Burroughs Medal for Nature Writing, and is elected to the American Academy of Arts and Letters

1955 Carson's third book, *The Edge of the Sea*, is published by Houghton Mifflin

1957 Marjorie Williams, Carson's niece, dies; Carson adopts her grandnephew, Roger, who turns five in February

1958 Maria Carson, Rachel's mother, dies in December at age 89

1960 Carson has a mastectomy and is sent home thinking the procedure was just a precaution

1962 Carson's fourth book, *Silent Spring*, is published by Houghton Mifflin; Carson and the book are both highly praised and highly criticized

President John F. Kennedy's Science Advisory Committee publishes a report that states Carson's claims in *Silent Spring* are accurate

1963 *CBS Reports* airs a television show, "The Silent Spring of Rachel Carson"; an estimated 10–15 million Americans watch it

1964 April 14, Rachel Carson dies in Silver Spring, Maryland, at age 56

1965 Carson's article "Help Your Child to Wonder," first published in 1956, is released posthumously as a book titled *The Sense of Wonder*

1972 DDT is banned from use in the United States; many other countries have already or will soon ban DDT

1980 President Jimmy Carter awards the Presidential Medal of Freedom to Carson; her grandnephew and son, Roger, accepts it for her

INTRODUCTION

A woman stands at the railing of a boat. She stares out at the sea, its surface gently ruffled by the breeze. She has been successful in so many ways: she works as a biologist in the government's fisheries department, she is the author of a book about the sea, and she has a close and loving family. But she's not entirely satisfied. She has always dreamed of being a full-time writer, yet publishing her first book a few years earlier left her disillusioned with writing books. Her education is in marine science, and her passions are birds and bird-watching, the ocean and shoreline exploring, the natural world and nature writing. What should her next move be? What's in her future?

Rachel Carson doesn't know it, but within a handful of years, hers will be a household name. She will become America's best-known nature writer. She will also struggle with family crises and her own worsening health. Through all this, she will question, and read, and write. Writing will often feel like she's swimming against schools of migrating fish, but eventually she will produce elegant sentences that stir the emotions and minds of millions of people. And, finally, she will publish a book that provokes a flood of fury, receives immense praise, and changes the world for the better.

A PATH TO BIOLOGY

> *"I can remember no time when I wasn't interested in the out-of-doors and the whole world of nature."*
> —Rachel Carson, in a speech, 1954

One May morning, about 100 years ago, a 14-year-old girl gathered her notebook, her camera, and a picnic lunch. She called to her dog, and together they set off through the grasses still adorned with dewdrops. They tramped away from the small Pennsylvania farmhouse where the girl lived with her family and followed a trail into the woods. Ever since she could remember, she had wandered through these woods, mostly with her mother. She could name the trees and the flowers, and she knew the birds by their songs, their markings, and even their nests.

Rachel at about age five reading *Little Folks* magazine to her dog, Candy. *Courtesy of Linda Lear Center for Special Collections and Archives, Connecticut College*

On this morning, the girl and her dog took a path up a hill. As they walked over pine needles carpeting the ground, the girl breathed in their pungent scent. She reveled in the stillness and the quiet. Ears at the ready, the girl heard a bird's call that sounded, she later wrote, like "witchery, witchery." She knew this bird—a Maryland yellow-throat—and she and the dog followed its call. The girl tiptoed through the trees, stopped to listen, walked on, listened again. Her patience paid off when she emerged into a sunny clearing and spotted a nest in some bushes. In the nest lay "four jewel-like eggs."

The girl, whose name was Rachel, wrote a story about that day of "bird's-nesting" in the woods, a day when she also found nests belonging to a bobwhite, an oriole, a cuckoo, a hummingbird, and an ovenbird. She sent her story to a children's publication called *St. Nicholas*. It was Rachel's fifth story printed in this magazine's pages, and her first one published about nature.

When this nature story came out, the year was 1922, and Rachel was on her way to becoming one of America's—and the world's—most recognized champions for nature and the environment. She became famous in an unusual way, particularly for a woman in the early 1900s. First, she became a biologist who studies nature, known today as an **ecologist**. Then she combined her knowledge of **ecology** with a passion for writing. Rachel used her skills to research complicated scientific ideas and then explain them in articles and books. Her writing captivated thousands of ordinary people with glimpses into nature's hidden worlds. With her final book—a wake-up call about humans meddling with nature—Rachel gave an unintentional boost to people trying to protect the environment. In this way, she helped inspire the **environmental movement** that continues today.

This story begins in Pennsylvania, on a hill overlooking the Allegheny River, in a woodland filled with singing birds, with Rachel Carson.

Rachel and Her Family

Rachel Louise Carson was born on a spring morning, May 27, 1907, the third child of Robert and Maria Carson. Rachel's older siblings, 10-year-old Marian and 8-year-old Robert, were both already attending school when Rachel came along. To 38-year-old Maria, Rachel was a gift. Maria had

Maria (McLean) Carson, Rachel's mother, and Robert Carson, Rachel's father. *Rachel Carson Papers, American Literature Collection, Beinecke Rare Book and Manuscript Library, Yale University*

a deep love of nature that her older children had never really shared. Rachel, Maria sensed, was different.

Born Maria McLean, Rachel's mother grew up in Washington, DC, where she did well at school, played piano, and sang beautifully. She attended college, and then worked as a schoolteacher and gave piano lessons. Maria also sang in the Washington Quintette Club, a group of five female singers.

Rachel's father, Robert Carson, was the eldest of six children. Little is known about Robert's early life, except that he sang in his church's choir. The winter when Robert was 30, he sang in a men's quartet at a choral gathering, where several groups were performing. One of them was the Washington Quintette Club. Robert met 25-year-old Maria, and they married the following year. Maria had to give up her teaching career; in the 1890s, married women were not allowed to teach.

Robert and Maria Carson lived for a few years in Canonsburg, Pennsylvania. By 1900, they had two children—Rachel's older siblings—and they moved to the town of Springdale. Springdale, home to about 1,200 people, lay alongside the Allegheny River. Robert Carson bought 64 acres of land on Colfax Hill with a four-room house perched near the hilltop. The house had no central heating and no indoor plumbing. The family pumped water from a well in front of the house and carried it in buckets to the house for cooking and washing. Maria gave birth to Rachel in this house seven years after they moved in. It would be home for Rachel throughout her childhood.

The Property on Colfax Hill

In 1900, the town of Springdale was growing. Industries were attracted to the area because steam-powered paddle-wheel boats could carry materials like iron, ore, logs, and oil down the Allegheny River to the city of Pittsburgh, 17 miles away. With industrial development came families, and with families came the need for homes and land.

When Robert Carson bought the large property on Colfax Hill for $11,000 (about $340,000 in today's money), his plan was to be a land developer. He subdivided parts of the property into lots and put them up for sale. Robert thought Springdale's economy would continue to grow and his

Baby Rachel with her brother, Robert, and sister, Marian. *Courtesy of Linda Lear Center for Special Collections and Archives, Connecticut College*

lots—for sale at $300 each—would sell quickly. But in the fall of 1907, a financial crisis hit the United States. Companies went bankrupt and people took their money out of banks. Buying land was the last thing on most people's minds.

Over the years, Robert sold only a few lots. He also worked as a traveling insurance salesman, but his income wasn't steady, since he got paid only when he made a sale. In later years, he worked as an electrician and at a power company.

Maria Carson contributed by teaching piano lessons to local children, but this didn't bring in much money, either. Financial struggle was a constant throughout Rachel's childhood. At times, money was so tight that the family couldn't even pay their milk bill.

The Wild Woods

The Carsons had little money, but they had lots of land covered in woods. With Marian and Robert at school all day, Maria took young Rachel outside to explore their surroundings. Together, mother and child wandered over the hills and under the trees. They smelled flowers, spotted insects, and listened for birds. Rachel learned the names of the plants and animals. She learned to observe the smallest of details. Spending a day wandering through the woods made her "gloriously happy," Rachel wrote as a teenager. Later in life, she described how

she had been "rather a solitary child and spent a great deal of time in woods and beside streams."

Even as Rachel tramped through nature and took delight in every discovery, she was aware of the industries surrounding her. At the base of Colfax Hill, Springdale became more and more industrial with a power company, a light company, and a glue factory. It was a dreary, grimy, smelly town. Rachel spent as much time as she could on her hill and in her woods.

A Writer Blooms

Rachel's love of nature was matched by her love of reading and writing. Among her favorite books as a child were Beatrix Potter's stories and Kenneth Grahame's *A Wind in the Willows*. One of Rachel's first surviving creations is a handmade booklet with illustrations of animals and a short verse about each one. Later, she wrote a story called "The Little Brown House" about two wrens looking for a house to live in.

At the age of 10, Rachel wrote a story about a Canadian pilot whom her brother, Robert, had mentioned in a letter home. Robert was away from home, serving in World War I with the US Army Air Service. Rachel submitted her story to a contest held by her favorite publication, *St. Nicholas*. Her mother wrote in the corner of the page to confirm that her daughter had written the story on her own.

Rachel was certain this story would launch her writing career, but she had to wait all summer to find out. Finally, issue number 45 of *St. Nicholas*

Maria Carson with her three children, Marian, Rachel, and Robert. *Rachel Carson Papers, American Literature Collection, Beinecke Rare Book and Manuscript Library, Yale University*

Experience Nature with Your Senses

Rachel Carson loved nothing better than to be out in nature. She had a particularly sharp eye and noticed all sorts of small details about the plants and animals she observed. These skills helped Rachel in her career as a biologist. Through careful observation, she learned how creatures connected with their surroundings and how their surroundings influenced them.

One of the best ways to observe and learn about the natural world can be to sit still and pay attention to what happens around you. Observing nature with your eyes is only one way to experience it. Smell, hearing, and touch are also powerful ways to learn about the world.

You'll Need

➤ Comfortable clothing suited to the climate and season

➤ Notepad and pencil

1. Go outside in your yard, a playground, or a park. Find a spot where you will feel comfortable sitting or standing for some time. Be still and quiet. Look at your surroundings. What do you see? Take notes or make drawings.

2. Close your eyes and listen. What sounds do you hear? From which directions do they come? How would you describe and spell those sounds?

3. Smell. Can you detect any scents? What do they remind you of?

4. Touch something near you. Perhaps a leaf, a seed pod, tree bark, or a rock. What is its texture? How would you describe it to someone who has never been to your part of the world?

5. When exploring nature, **do not** use the fifth sense, taste. Some leaves, berries, and other plant parts have dangerous toxins in them.

6. Make notes about what you have observed. Which sense gives you the most information? Which sense do you enjoy using the most? Which sense surprised you?

7. Think about connections between some of the things you noticed. Why is a particular plant, animal, or rock in the spot it's in? How did it get there? How does it interact with other things at that location? Does it relate to your world?

Optional: Return to your nature spot in another season or visit spots in different environments. Repeat your observations and compare between the seasons or the locations. How are they similar? How do they differ? Do you prefer one to the other?

(left) **Rachel at about age 10 with brother, Robert, in his air service uniform and sister, Marian.** *Carson family, by permission of Rachel Carson Council, Inc.*

(right) *St. Nicholas* **magazine was published from 1873 to 1943.** *Photo by Rowena Rae, courtesy Rachel Carson Homestead, Springdale, Pennsylvania*

arrived. Rachel opened the pages, and sure enough, her story had made it into print. The headline read: A BATTLE IN THE CLOUDS BY RACHEL L. CARSON (AGE 10). And there was more: her story had won a silver badge! Thrilled by her success, Rachel got straight to work writing another story to enter into the next contest.

Over the next few years, Rachel submitted more stories to *St. Nicholas* magazine and saw her stories and name printed in the magazine five times. Her stories earned her a gold badge and the title of Honor Member, which came with $10.

She started submitting stories to other magazines too. Rachel had caught the writing bug that would shape the rest of her life.

School Years

Rachel attended School Street School in Springdale. She earned high grades, yet she missed a lot of school days. Sometimes Rachel was absent from school for weeks on end. Maria frequently kept Rachel home and tutored her daughter herself, sometimes because of poor weather, sometimes because of the threat of infectious diseases like measles and whooping cough, and perhaps sometimes just for the joy of spending time with her bright daughter. During these homeschooling periods, Rachel read, and read, and read. She particularly enjoyed reading stories and poems about the ocean, even though she had never seen the sea. She read Herman Melville, author of *Moby Dick* and other sea adventures, and Robert Louis Stevenson, author of *Treasure Island*.

The long periods of missed school didn't do much to help Rachel make friends. In fact, she had only a few friends, and even they visited her home infrequently. The Carson house was some distance from the center of town, and Rachel also felt embarrassed by her family's humble home. Maria didn't encourage Rachel's friends to come over, either. Rachel seemed content with her quiet life and soaked up her surroundings.

School Street School went only to 10th grade, so for two years, Rachel attended Parnassus High School in a town two miles away. She traveled back and forth by trolley every day. In May 1928, a few days before turning 18, Rachel graduated from 12th grade. In the school yearbook, the editors wrote a poem to accompany the photo of each graduating student. The poem next to Rachel's photo read:

> *Rachel's like the mid-day sun*
> *Always very bright*
> *Never stops her studying*
> *'till she gets it right.*

Rachel graduated as the top student in her class.

College in Pittsburgh

Maria Carson insisted that Rachel go to college, and that was fine by Rachel. In fact, it was more than fine, because Rachel craved further study. Gaining admission to Pennsylvania College for Women, or PCW (today called Chatham University), was easy. Rachel even received a scholarship

INFECTIOUS DISEASES AND VACCINES

Rachel Carson's mother frequently kept her daughter home when an infectious disease was circulating. Infectious diseases are caused by viruses, bacteria, and other germs that can be spread from person to person by sneezing, coughing, sharing drink containers, and sometimes even touching the same surfaces. A century ago, diseases like measles, polio, and whooping cough claimed thousands of lives every year in the United States (and worldwide).

There was no prevention until scientists learned how to make vaccines. Vaccines allow the body to develop germ-fighting tools called antibodies. Antibodies give a person immunity, or protection, so that when disease germs enter the body, the antibodies recognize and destroy them. By the 1960s, several vaccines were available. Some diseases, like polio, have been eradicated, or stamped out from the United States (but still exist in some countries). Smallpox has been eradicated from the entire world.

When most people in a community have immunity, there is little chance of the disease spreading. When too few people are immune, a disease can sweep from one vulnerable person to the next.

(left) **A depiction of steel factories at night in the town of Duquesne, near Pittsburgh, Pennsylvania, in 1900.** *North Wind Picture Archives/Alamy Stock Photo*

(right) **Grace Croff, English professor at Pennsylvania College for Women, and Rachel sitting in the grounds.** *Courtesy of Linda Lear Center for Special Collections and Archives, Connecticut College*

to pay for part of the tuition. Maria and Robert planned to take a bank loan and sell some of their land to pay the rest of Rachel's expenses. As before, however, the land sales didn't go too well. Maria had to teach more piano students to bring in extra cash. She also sold apples, chickens, and even the Carsons' china dishes.

When Rachel began college in September 1925, it was a big change for her. She lived in a dormitory and had a roommate. She was also now in a large city—Pittsburgh in the 1920s had a population of more than half a million people. And, as the iron and steel capital of the world, it was a dirty city too. These industries spewed pollution into the air. Ash dusted everything and sometimes blocked the sunshine. It was a far cry from her woodland home in Springdale, but Rachel had a mission: she

wanted to earn her bachelor's degree in English and become a writer.

Professor Grace Croff taught Rachel English composition. Within a few months, Miss Croff became Rachel's mentor and friend. When classes finished for the day, the two women frequently chatted together over tea or on a wooden bench out in the college grounds. Rachel impressed Miss Croff with her writing during that first year. One of her stories, called "The Master of the Ship's Light," described the ocean and the coast with vivid language, even though Rachel had still not seen the sea. One of Miss Croff's comments about this ocean-themed story noted how well Rachel translated complex information into an engaging story. This ability served her throughout her career.

Rachel earned high grades in her first year, but she kept very much to herself and made few friends. In part, she was driven to study and learn the craft of writing. In part, she was self-confident and independent, which many of the other girls took as her being a bit unfriendly. She also had severe acne and thick, greasy hair. Although Rachel rarely attended tea parties or dances put on by the college or other schools, she did participate in some parts of college life. She played on the grass hockey team, went to the junior prom, and occasionally joined informal social occasions. One time, on a snowy winter evening, Rachel went sledding in the dark with a group of girls, then came back inside to sit around a fire and have a late-night feast. Rachel remembered it as one of the best evenings she spent at college.

To make social matters trickier, Rachel's mother visited her at the college nearly every Saturday. During these visits, Maria was interested only in Rachel. Mother and daughter would read together at the library or sit on Rachel's bed eating homemade cookies. Sometimes Maria typed Rachel's essays and stories, a task Maria took on for the rest of her life.

Rachel seemed not to mind her mother's frequent visits. Maria had been Rachel's closest companion all her childhood. This companionship continued throughout her adulthood too. Rachel also knew how much her mother had sacrificed so that she could attend college. It seemed only fair that her mother should have the chance to enjoy some of the college atmosphere.

A Family Full of Tension

Maria Carson's regular weekend visits to Rachel gave her a break from family in Springdale. Rachel's sister, Marian, had married when Rachel was just eight years old and divorced three years later. By the time Rachel started college, Marian and her second husband had an infant daughter, a second child on the way, and a marriage in tatters. Rachel's brother, Robert, was also in a tense marriage and had a fussy, teething baby.

When Rachel arrived home in June after her first year at college, she faced a summer in a crowded, noisy house. Nine people lived under the one roof that summer: Rachel; her father and mother; her brother with his wife and infant daughter; and her sister with her daughters, one a toddler and the other an infant. Rachel did her

Rachel, second from the right in the back row, with the grass hockey team at Pennsylvania College for Women. *Chatham University Archives and Special Collections*

Write a Haiku

Rachel Carson read poetry as a child and throughout her time at Pennsylvania College for Women. She also wrote some poems. There are many different forms used for poems, and one that's known for focusing on the natural world is haiku, which originated in Japan.

A traditional Japanese haiku focuses on the emotion of a single moment or on describing an image with the senses. It has three short lines with 17 syllables in a 5-7-5 pattern (first and last lines have five syllables each, and the middle line has seven syllables).

Here's an example of a haiku I wrote in August 2018 when acres and acres of the province where I live were burning:

> *Neon orange sun,*
> *Hangs limp in the sullen sky.*
> *Forest fires rampage.*

Here it is again with the syllables divided by slashes:

> *Ne/on/ or/ange/ sun*
> *Hangs/ limp/ in/ the/ sul/len/ sky.*
> *For/est/ fires/ ram/page.*

Try your hand at writing a haiku.

You'll Need

➤ Paper and pencil

1. Write down a list of things that interest you about nature—animals, plants, seasons, or scenes.

2. Choose one of the topics on your list and write down words that describe or relate to that subject. Think of verbs (action words), adjectives (descriptive words), and emotions.

3. Start writing the first line of the haiku. Aim for vivid description and words that awaken the senses.

4. Continue with the second line. Read your words aloud and tap out the syllables to help with counting them.

5. Write the last line. Try to add a twist or revelation with this last line or evoke a new emotion for the reader.

6. When you're happy with your haiku, write it out in good copy and share it with family or classmates.

best to help care for her three young nieces, but she escaped when she could to wander her beloved woods. Finally, September arrived and Rachel could return to Pittsburgh.

An Introduction to Biology

During her second year, Rachel enrolled in another writing class with Miss Croff. She also registered for a biology class, since the college required every student to take at least one science course. Introductory biology was taught by Professor Mary Scott Skinker, a dynamic, glamorous woman who expected much of her students. Many students avoided Miss Skinker's class because of her demanding standards. Yet, students who worked hard received a lot of her time and encouragement, even if they weren't particularly good at biology.

Rachel loved learning and studying, worked very hard, and was also extremely good at biology. Her curiosity and deep knowledge of natural history impressed Miss Skinker. The professor's positive feedback and attention fed Rachel's growing passion for biology. Rachel stayed after class to ask questions—she wanted to know everything Miss Skinker knew. This biology class and its dynamic teacher had opened a new window for Rachel. Through it, she saw another way to immerse herself in the natural world she loved so dearly.

The Biology of Nature

Rachel didn't know it, but she had fallen in love with a type of biology called ecology. Ecology is the scientific study of how plants and animals interact with each other and with their surroundings. Ecologists are the scientists who do this work to find out why and how **organisms**—all living things—live where they do.

In the early 1900s, however, ecology was in its infancy, and the words *ecology* and *ecologist* were not common. Rachel didn't describe herself as an ecologist, but she wrote again and again about one of ecology's basic concepts: everything in nature connects to something else in nature. All the plants and animals living and connecting in a particular area—plus all the physical features of that area like soil, rocks, and water—form an **ecosystem**. An ecosystem can be large, like a whole forest or a great lake, or it can be small, like a fallen log or a single tide pool. Every organism—whether it's a plant or an animal—needs a place to live, food to eat, and certain conditions in which to grow, live, and reproduce. All these things together allow an organism to occupy a **niche** (pronounced either "neesh" or "nitch"). A niche can be thought of as an organism's role or job in its ecosystem.

Every time Rachel walked in the woods near her family's home, she would have seen examples of connections between one organism and another, and between organisms and their environment. For example, she might have seen moss using a rock as its place to live, a rabbit eating grasses to survive and grow, a bird gathering

Mary Scott Skinker, biology professor at Pennsylvania College for Women. *Chatham University Archives and Special Collections*

twigs to build its nest, or a fox catching a mouse to feed to its kits. Rachel's childhood explorations of nature gave her an instinctive understanding of how plants and animals connected to each other and their surroundings. Studying biology with Miss Skinker gave Rachel an opportunity to find out how and why those connections worked, to understand the inner workings of ecosystems.

A Difficult Choice

Despite her newfound love of biology, Rachel never lost her ambition to write. She joined the staffs of the college's student newspaper, the *Arrow*, and its literary publication, the *Englicode*. Miss Croff acted as advisor to these publications and encouraged Rachel not only to join them but to write for them. Rachel published numerous stories in the *Englicode* during her college years, including one story that won the college's Omega literary prize.

Toward the end of her second year of college, Rachel began to realize that she was leaning more toward studying biology than English. She found herself facing a dilemma: should she continue as an English major and become a writer, or should she switch to biology and become a scientist? In the 1920s, the humanities and the sciences were separate fields. Rachel had to choose one path or the other.

One stormy night, Rachel sat alone in her dorm room reading a poem assigned by Miss Croff. The poem had been written nearly a century earlier by Alfred Lord Tennyson, a British poet. As the wind whooshed around the old, brick building and rattled its windows, Rachel read the long poem. She came to its last line: "For the mighty wind arises, roaring seaward, and I go."

The words flooded Rachel with emotion. Years later, she recalled that experience in a letter to a friend. "That line spoke to something within me," she wrote. "My own destiny was somehow linked with the sea."

Rachel chose to major in biology.

A Hard Path to Follow

Miss Skinker was delighted with Rachel's decision to pursue biology. The friendship that had already begun between the two of them blossomed. It was a friendship and mentorship that lasted until Mary Skinker's death many years later.

Rachel's third year at college was filled with science classes, and to Rachel's delight, field trips. Miss Skinker frequently took her students to Wildwood, a rural area with ponds and streams, to observe nature and collect specimens. Rachel's passion for nature was equaled by her teacher's. They also shared a desire to safeguard nature and allow it to stay wild.

Toward the end of Rachel's third year at college, she learned with dismay that Miss Skinker was taking a leave from teaching to complete her doctoral degree. In the 1920s and 1930s, becoming a scientist was a struggle for women. Science was seen as a man's profession. Those women who did stick with their studies and complete a science degree often had great difficulty moving into a career, and many of them became teachers at women's colleges. Mary Skinker had become a teacher at PCW after earning her master's degree, and during summer breaks she took courses toward a doctoral degree at Johns Hopkins University. Now she decided that to move forward in her career, she needed to complete that degree.

Rachel's first thought on hearing Miss Skinker's news was to enroll at Johns Hopkins University herself. Even though she had completed only three of four years at PCW, Rachel applied to enter Johns Hopkins as a master's degree student. She got accepted! But there was a catch: students who were admitted to the master's program without a bachelor's degree paid higher tuition. Rachel and her family already had tight finances. They owed PCW more than $1,500 (about $22,000 in today's dollars). Paying even more money to attend Johns Hopkins University was out of the question.

Rachel resigned herself to staying at PCW for one more year. To add to Rachel's disappointment, Miss Croff also left her teaching position. Rachel worked diligently through her fourth-year studies, learning as much as she could from the replacement biology teacher, Dr. Anna Whiting. It became clear very quickly that Whiting's passion lay in an entirely different field than Miss Skinker's. Whiting had earned her doctoral degree in cattle breeding, and she had little training in the life sciences and no interest in field work. Rachel fretted that she would not receive the training necessary to pursue a higher degree in biology.

Nevertheless, during her fourth year, Rachel reapplied to Johns Hopkins University in the hope

of being able to start a master's degree the following September. Again, the university accepted her. This time, thanks in part to a letter of support written by Mary Skinker, Rachel received a scholarship for her entire tuition. Rachel's proud mother made sure that PCW's newspaper published the news.

By the time Rachel Carson completed her studies and graduated from PCW in June 1929, she was ready to leave industrial Pittsburgh and head east. That change would bring her closer to the sea and closer to her dream of becoming a biologist.

One of Rachel's yearbook photos at Pennsylvania College for Women. *Chatham University Archives & Special Collections*

2

RACHEL SEES THE SEA

"There was nothing, really, for human words to say in the presence of something so vast, mysterious and immensely powerful." —Rachel Carson writing about standing at the ocean's edge in "Our Ever-Changing Shore," *Holiday*, 1958

Rachel Carson set off from Springdale in July 1929 for adventures that would take her farther from her family than she'd ever been before. Weekend visits from her mother would no longer be possible. She traveled first to Baltimore to find a room near the Homewood campus of Johns Hopkins University. Classes didn't start until October, but she wanted to enjoy her summer knowing she had a place to live when she began her master of science degree.

Carson sitting on the deck of a research boat at Woods Hole, Massachusetts. *Mary Frye/By permission of Rachel Carson Council, Inc.*

Carson's next stop was a visit with her former teacher, now dear friend, Mary Skinker, in Virginia. The trip to Skinker's family cabin entailed two bus rides, a taxicab ride, and finally a horseback ride for four miles up a mountainside. For a 22-year-old who had never traveled far from home, let alone to unknown destinations by herself, this journey must have been a little nerve-wracking, and perhaps also exhilarating. After several joyful days of hiking and talking together, Carson and Skinker descended the mountain and took a bus to Washington, DC. Carson said goodbye and boarded a train bound for New York City and her first glimpse of the sea.

A Summer of Delights

On an evening late in July, Carson set foot on a passenger boat that took her to New Bedford,

Massachusetts. There, she transferred to another boat and steamed to Woods Hole. In a letter to a friend, Carson described her first experience of the sea as "glorious."

Woods Hole is home to the Marine Biological Laboratory, first established in 1888 and still going strong today. Carson had been accepted to spend six weeks there that summer as a beginning investigator. Unlike many research institutes in the 1920s, the Marine Biological Laboratory treated men and women as equals, though men vastly outnumbered women there. The laboratory encouraged cooperation among its researchers, whether male or female, fully trained biologist or budding student. It was a place for like-minded people with a passion for biology to discuss ideas and work on scientific problems.

Carson worked in a laboratory in the Crane building, tasked with figuring out what her research project would be for her master's degree. She spent a great deal of time in the library and eventually settled on a project: she would compare a brain nerve in lizards and snakes to see if the nerve looked and worked the same way in each of these reptiles. This type of research is called a comparative study and requires careful dissection and work with a microscope.

Early on, Carson doubted her skills. She feared the poor biology instruction during her final year of college had left her unprepared to do the work needed for a comparative study. Over the summer, the cooperation at the laboratory gave her new confidence. Carson's time in Woods Hole included more than just library research and microscope

A postcard from the 1920s of the Marine Biological Laboratory and surroundings, Woods Hole, Massachusetts. *Woods Hole Historical Museum*

work. She met and talked with the faculty and other students, went on boat trips up and down the bay to dredge plants and animals from the seabed, and spent a day on a government research ship collecting organisms from the deep sea. She even tried learning how to swim.

One of Carson's college friends, Mary Frye, was also in Woods Hole and together they spent hours wandering the seashore at low tide, examining tide-pool creatures like sea anemones and urchins. On nights with a full moon, they went to the dock to watch worms wriggling together as they mated.

Carson was enthralled by the sounds, the smells, the sights—by everything to do with the sea. That sense of wonder at the ocean's creatures and its many mysteries remained with her for the rest of her life.

The Nature of Ecosystems

As Carson explored the tide pools, she encountered both **biotic** (living) things and **abiotic** (nonliving) things. All ecosystems, no matter how small or large, contain living organisms like bacteria, fungi, plants, and animals as well as nonliving factors like sunlight, water, air, and soil. The organisms interact with their physical and chemical surroundings, which make up their **habitat**— the place where they live.

Carson saw firsthand how anemones find secure footholds on the rocks forming tide pools. She noticed seaweeds being dappled by sunlight, giving them energy for **photosynthesis**. She

marveled at the fragile bodies of jellyfish suspended in and supported by water. None of these organisms could live as they do without the abiotic parts of their ecosystem.

The organisms in an ecosystem form a **community** of members interacting with each other. An anemone waves its fingerlike tentacles to create tiny water currents that sweep small, floating creatures near enough for the anemone to snatch and eat. A fish darts beneath a seaweed frond to avoid capture by a seabird. A squid spurts ink to cloud the water and escape its **predator**. These interactions show how everything in nature is connected to something else. In all her writing, Carson stressed the connections in nature. When something happens to one organism or one part of an ecosystem, other organisms and other parts of the ecosystem will be affected.

For example, think of adult Pacific salmon migrating from the ocean into a river and swimming miles and miles upriver to lay their eggs. Once they've spawned, the salmon die, and their bodies become a feast for all kinds of other organisms: bears, eagles, insects, and bacteria. Now imagine that a rock slide blocks the river. When fall comes, the salmon can't swim up the river to spawn, and they die miles before their destination. All the creatures upstream that fed on the salmon carcasses in previous years must find something else to eat. They might then grow less, have fewer babies, or migrate, all because something happened somewhere else in their ecosystem. Carson once wrote about this exact scenario happening to Pacific salmon in British Columbia. "In 1913," she

Make Birdseed Cookies

You can help birds get a belly full of food by hanging bird feeders outside, especially in winter. Although you can buy all sorts of different bird feeders, you can also make some with just a few ingredients.

You'll Need

- 6–8 cookie cutters
- Baking tray
- Wax paper (optional)
- 1 tablespoon of vegetable oil (or non-stick cooking spray)
- 1 packet of unflavored gelatin
- 2 tablespoons of cold water
- ⅓ cup of boiling water
- 2 cups of birdseed (any seeds are fine, although small ones like nyjer, milo, millet, and hulled sunflower seeds work best)
- Spoon
- Skewer or toothpick
- String or yarn
- 6–8 twigs or thin sticks, about 6 inches long

1. Place cookie cutters on a baking tray (with or without a layer of wax paper) and coat the inside edges with vegetable oil or nonstick cooking spray.
2. Combine gelatin with cold water, stir, and let sit for about a minute.
3. Add boiling water to the gelatin and stir until dissolved.
4. Add birdseed to the gelatin and mix until all seeds are coated.
5. Spoon the seed mixture into the cookie cutters and press firmly.
6. Make a small hole in each cookie with the skewer or toothpick.
7. Refrigerate for 2–3 hours or overnight until the seed mixture has set.
8. Bring the cookies out and let them warm to room temperature.
9. Gently push the cookies out of the cookie cutters and thread each cookie with a string or piece of yarn.
10. Poke a twig or small stick through the hole to give birds a perch.

11. Hang the cookies from tree branches or a hook outside your window.

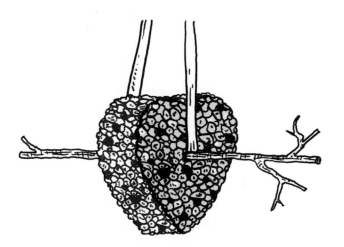

12. Enjoy watching birds appreciate your birdseed cookies!

Note: If you make extra cookies and want to save some to hang out at a later time, keep the extras in the fridge, or even in the freezer, so they don't get moldy.

wrote, "rock slides on the Fraser River 130 miles from the sea, in a narrow passage known as Hell's Gate, prevented millions of fish from reaching their spawning grounds. This disaster not only virtually destroyed a complete cycle of fish, but created an obstruction for future runs."

All her life, Carson thought about nature's connections and the consequences of altering or breaking those connections.

The Master's Student

At the end of her summer at Woods Hole, Carson took a short trip back to Springdale to visit her family. Then she got settled in her Baltimore lodgings and started at Professor Rheinart Cowles's zoology lab in Gilman Hall at Johns Hopkins University. In her first year, Carson took various science classes—botany, physiology, genetics, and organic chemistry. In the biology department, there were about three male students to every one female student. In one of her chemistry classes, Carson was one of only two women among 70 students. But Carson was undaunted. She spent as much time as she could working in the lab on her project.

Carson's lab work didn't go very well, though. She struggled to get enough useful data from the dissections of reptile nerves for her comparative study. She changed her research project to pit viper snakes to study the depression—the pit—on either side of the creature's head. When that project faltered, she started studying squirrel embryos—the early stages when unborn animals are developing. But the adult squirrels wouldn't mate to produce

(left) **Carson's entrance photo at Johns Hopkins University, 1929.** *Carson family/By permission of Rachel Carson Council, Inc.*

(right) **Gilman Hall, the building where Rachel spent much of her time while studying at Johns Hopkins University.** *Rowena Rae*

the embryos she needed. Carson sent a letter to a friend telling of her frustration but also showing her sense of humor by writing that without the squirrel embryos she had nothing to study, which was "the situation in a nutshell." Eventually, Professor Cowles suggested that Rachel study the urinary system in fish. This project worked.

The Great Depression Interferes

The struggles Rachel had with her lab work during her master's degree weren't the only stresses in her life during those years. The Great Depression created widespread unemployment and financial insecurity, so Carson's family moved from Springdale to Baltimore in early 1930 in the hope of finding more work. They rented a house—one with indoor plumbing, though no central heating—on the outskirts of the city, in a rural area to the northeast.

Carson moved into the house with her mother and father. Her twice-divorced sister, Marian, and two nieces also moved in later in the year. Even her brother, Robert, moved into the house for a short time, in early 1931. He found a job in Baltimore but didn't contribute much financially to the household. One time he got paid in cats, bringing home a Persian and her three kittens. Although Carson had grown up with dogs as pets, she fell in love with these furry bundles. For the rest of her life, she shared her home with cats.

The first summer after starting at Johns Hopkins, Carson helped teach summer biology classes to earn some money. But even with this income and a scholarship, she and her family didn't have enough money for her to attend university full-time in the fall. Carson had no choice but to enroll as a part-time student and get a part-time job. For one year, she worked as a lab assistant in the university's medical school, and the next year she taught biology at the University of Maryland's dental school.

Carson finished her degree only a year behind schedule, receiving her master of science degree in June 1932. She then enrolled at the university as a doctoral student to earn a PhD. This time, her research project involved a tank full of eels. She was fascinated with their life cycle; they grow up in freshwater streams and then swim far into the salty ocean to reproduce. Carson planned to investigate how these long, serpentlike fish manage the lifestyle change from living in freshwater to living in salt water during their **migration**.

For the next two years, Carson kept up her doctoral work, but money was a constant struggle. Her sister became diabetic and often couldn't work. Her brother had work only occasionally (though he did move into his own place). A neighbor later remembered dropping by one time at the dinner hour and seeing the Carson family sitting at the table with nothing more to eat than a bowl of apples.

Sadness at Home

During the early 1930s, friends who visited the Carson family home saw how devoted Carson and her mother were to each other. The close bond they had formed during Carson's childhood and college years would continue for the rest of their lives. One friend also noted that Carson's father

THE GREAT DEPRESSION

The Great Depression is the name given to a period in the 1930s and early 1940s when countries around the world experienced severe economic downturns. The economies in the United States, Canada, Europe, and elsewhere went into a terrible slump. In the fall of 1929, money lost its value, hundreds of banks and businesses closed, and people lost their jobs. At the Great Depression's worst, nearly one quarter of working-age adults in America couldn't find a job. Families lost their homes and didn't have enough money to buy food. At the same time, farmers in the southwestern Great Plains couldn't grow crops or raise animals because of a series of severe droughts and dust storms known as the Dust Bowl. Many of them abandoned their farms.

This trouble in the US economy affected international trade, which is all the importing and exporting of goods between countries. The economic crisis came to an end during World War II (1939–1945), when there was demand for products to fight the war. Factories opened and people went back to work. When the United States joined the fighting in 1941, young men were drafted into military service. Whether at home or overseas, millions of Americans were working again, making money, and able to feed their families.

Soil from Dust Bowl winds piled against farm buildings in the 1930s.
Arthur Rothstein/Library of Congress Prints and Photographic Division

Chart Bird Migrations

Animal migration fascinated Rachel Carson. She wrote about bird, fish, and insect migrations during her life. Animal migration is one of the many spectacular and sometimes mysterious events in nature.

Around the globe, scientists have identified major pathways or flyways that migrating birds use to travel between their winter feeding grounds and summer breeding grounds. Many birds travel in only a portion of a flyway and others go through more than one flyway during their migrations. However, the flyway concept helps scientists and other people study birds' migratory pathways and habitat needs. The map here shows the four North American flyways: Pacific, Central, Mississippi, and Atlantic.

Examples of migratory birds in North America are:

Calliope hummingbird   *Indigo bunting*   *Mountain plover*   *Rusty blackbird*   *Tundra swan*
Harris's sparrow   *Marbled godwit*   *Purple sandpiper*   *Sedge wren*   *Yellow-bellied sapsucker*

You'll Need

➤ Photocopy of the map shown here, or search the Internet for "North America flyway" maps and print one of the maps you find

➤ Six colored markers or pencils (three colors with a dark and light shade of each)

➤ Library or Internet access

1. Use a field guide to North American birds or a website such as the Cornell Lab of Ornithology's All About Birds (www.allaboutbirds.org) to look up three of the migratory birds listed above, or find the names of other migratory bird species.

2. For each species, look at a range map to find the location of its winter (feeding) and summer (breeding) grounds. Use a dark shade of one color (for example, dark blue) to mark the winter territory on your flyways map and a light shade of the same color (for example, light blue) to mark the summer territory. Use a different color for each species.

3. Which flyway or flyways does each species use? Do some species overlap? Do any of the species spend time in habitats in your state or province?

Optional: Research the species you mapped to find out which habitats—such as wetland, grassland, rocky shore—they spend time in during winter and summer, and during their migration stopovers (the times when they land to feed or rest along their migration route).

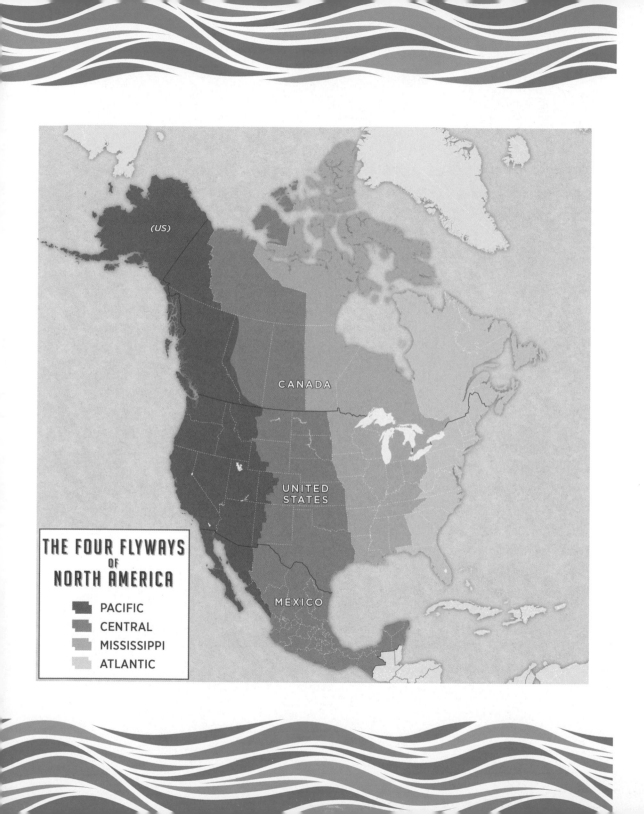

THE FOUR FLYWAYS
OF
NORTH AMERICA

- ■ PACIFIC
- ■ CENTRAL
- ■ MISSISSIPPI
- ■ ATLANTIC

looked ill, though Carson never mentioned his health in any of her letters to friends.

By 1934, the family's finances were so desperate that Carson decided she had no choice but to withdraw from the doctoral program and get a full-time job. She kept teaching biology at the dental school while searching for a full-time teaching position. She was willing to move to any of the eastern states, but the Great Depression meant very few jobs were available.

During this tense time, Carson did two things that would influence the rest of her life. First, she pulled out some of the poems and short stories she'd written at college, revised them, and submitted them to various magazines. Although the magazines rejected every single one, Carson had reawakened her love of writing. Second, on her friend Mary Skinker's urging, Carson took the exams that would allow her to apply for science jobs in the federal government. She took one exam in January 1935 and two in May, and she passed them all.

As if life weren't tough enough for the Carson family that year, in July, Carson's father went into the back garden for some fresh air, collapsed, and died. Robert Carson was 71. Maria arranged for her husband's body to be sent to Canonsburg, Pennsylvania, for burial in a family plot. Money was so tight that Carson, her siblings, and her mother couldn't afford to travel and attend the burial.

Carson, now age 28, grieved for her father and took over the role of head of the household. She had to earn enough money to look after herself and her mother, as well as help support her sister and two nieces.

3

WRITING ABOUT THE OCEAN

"To sense this world of waters known to the creatures of the sea we must shed our human perceptions . . . and enter vicariously into a universe of all-pervading water." —Rachel Carson, "Undersea," 1937

A few months after her father's death, Rachel Carson sat in the office of a government biologist. Elmer Higgins worked for the US Bureau of Fisheries, and Carson had gone to meet him on the advice of her friend Mary Skinker. Carson asked if Higgins's department had any jobs available. He said it didn't, but he did have a problem that perhaps she could take off his hands: an assignment given to his department to write scripts for 52 radio segments about marine life. Higgins's staff knew all about

Carson bird-watching at Woods Hole, Massachusetts. *Shirley A. Briggs/By permission of Rachel Carson Council, Inc.*

marine life, but they couldn't make it interesting for a public audience. He needed someone who understood marine biology and who could also write well.

Carson fit the bill. She later recalled, "He talked to me for a few minutes and then said: 'I've never seen a written word of yours, but I'm going to take a sporting chance.'" He hired Carson to write the radio scripts.

Something to Write About

The project's official title was Romance Under the Waters, but everyone in Higgins's office called the radio scripts "seven-minute fish tales," since each one was to run for seven minutes on the air. Carson traveled twice a week by bus to the Bureau of Fisheries office in Washington, DC, to write the scripts. She earned $6.50 per day. For eight months, she continued writing the scripts, which aired weekly on the CBS Radio Network. People liked the radio segments, and by the time the project ended, Higgins knew the chance he'd taken by hiring Carson had been a good one.

Next, Higgins asked Carson to write an essay about marine life, something that could be used for a government brochure. Carson agreed and set to work. In April 1936, she handed Higgins an essay titled "The World of Waters." Higgins read it while Carson sat on the other side of the desk in his crowded office. Carson later described his reaction: "My chief handed it back with a twinkle in his eye. 'I don't think it will do,' he said. 'Better try again.'" But then he added, "Send this one to the *Atlantic*."

The *Atlantic* was—and still is—a highly respected literary magazine published in Boston. Carson must have been pleased by Higgins's warm approval of her essay. She made a few changes to it and sent it out, but not to the *Atlantic Monthly* (its full name at that time). Instead, she submitted it to a *Reader's Digest* magazine contest with a $1,000 prize. Her family sorely needed that money, but Carson never heard back from the magazine about her entry.

While she was working on the essay for Higgins, Carson started writing articles about marine life and sending them to the *Baltimore Sun*, the city newspaper. The first article she submitted described the shad fishery and how the population of these silvery fish was declining. The *Sun* accepted the article and paid Carson $20 for it. It was published on March 1, 1936, with the title "It'll Be Shad-Time Soon." Carson could now call herself a paid science writer.

Over the next few years, Carson submitted and published several newspaper articles about subjects such as tuna fishing, oyster farming, duck populations, and eel migration. Each article brought in $10 or $20.

Years later, recalling her difficult decision in college to switch her major from English to biology, Carson said, "I had given up writing forever, I thought. It never occurred to me that I was merely getting something to write about." That's exactly what she'd done, though. Her knowledge of marine life, her enjoyment of reading scientific papers, and her wonderment at the ocean came together beautifully with her skill as a writer.

Elmer Higgins hired Carson to write radio scripts for the US Bureau of Fisheries. *NOAA Fisheries*

A Full-Time Job

That summer, a position came up at the Bureau of Fisheries for a junior aquatic biologist. Carson applied and got it—a full-time job, at last! In this position, Carson was one of only two women with professional jobs (rather than administrative jobs) at the bureau. Her job involved examining data, gathering information from fish biologists and other experts, and writing reports and brochures. She spent time in the lab, the library, and the field, and all the while, she collected ideas for newspaper articles. Nearly every week she sent an article idea to the editor at the *Baltimore Sun*. He liked many of them. Before writing an article, Carson read as much as she could find about the topic and contacted scientists to answer her questions. She also visited Chesapeake Bay to see the different areas firsthand and talk with people who fished or worked on the water.

Together, her government job and article research gave Carson opportunities to learn more and more about marine and shore ecosystems. They also meant she didn't have to worry so much about money. But this freedom from financial anxiety didn't last for long.

More Sadness at Home

In January 1937, Carson's sister, Marian, died of pneumonia (a lung infection) at age 40. Carson, only 29 years old, and her mother, now in her late 60s, took over the full-time care of Marian's two daughters, 12-year-old Virginia and 11-year-old

Marjorie. The girls' father didn't have the means to care for and raise his daughters. Besides, Carson and Maria loved the two girls and were the only family the girls knew. Carson continued her role as breadwinner and Maria did the cooking and housework as she always had.

Carson now had full financial responsibility for a family of four—a rare situation for a young woman in the 1930s. She also had decisions to help make about her nieces' upbringing. One of her first decisions was to move the family to a neighborhood with good schools for the girls and easier access to her work. She rented a house in Silver Spring, a community between Baltimore and Washington, DC, and the family moved in July.

Carson also decided to try selling the essay that Elmer Higgins had rejected for the government brochure but had clearly liked as a piece of writing. She revised "The World of Waters" and submitted it in June to the *Atlantic Monthly*. A month later, she got a positive response, and before the summer was out she had received the payment of $100. The article appeared in the magazine's September issue with the title "Undersea."

A Writer of Interest

One reaction to "Undersea" came from an unexpected source. Carson received a letter from Quincy Howe, an editor at Simon & Schuster, one of the big book publishing companies. Howe asked whether Carson had thought of writing a book about the sea, and she replied to say no but the idea intrigued her. It turns out that another

Carson's staff photo at the Bureau of Fisheries. *US Fish and Wildlife Service*

Create a Sound Map

Bird-watching was a hobby for Rachel Carson throughout her life. As well as looking for birds, bird-watchers listen for them and can often recognize a species from its call. Listening to birds and other sounds in nature provides another way to enjoy and appreciate your surroundings. In this activity, you will create a sound map.

You'll Need

➤ Comfortable clothing
➤ Paper and pencil

1. Go outside in your yard, a playground, or a park. Find a spot where you can stand or sit comfortably for up to five minutes.

2. Draw a large circle that fills most of the page. Draw a line from the circle's top to bottom and another line from the left side to the right side, as shown in the diagram. Where the two lines cross at the center of the circle, make a small X. The X represents you.

3. Stay still and listen. Close your eyes if it helps you concentrate.

4. Whenever you hear a sound, make a mark on your page to show which direction the sound came from and approximately how far away it was. Make just a few marks to represent the sound you heard, not a detailed picture. The idea is to focus on listening, not get absorbed in drawing. For example, you might represent a bird's chirp with a musical note. The wind rustling leaves might be a wavy line.

5. Keep listening and marking sounds for 3–5 minutes.

6. When you're ready to stop, draw a legend in a blank spot on your map. A legend tells a viewer what each mark means, as shown in the diagram. Also write down your location, the time of day, and the date on your sound map.

7. What more do you now know about the spot you chose that you didn't know before you began?

8. If others did the activity at the same time as you, compare your sound maps. Did you all hear the same things coming from the same direction?

Optional: Return to the same spot in different seasons or at different times of day. Compare new sound maps with ones you created previously.

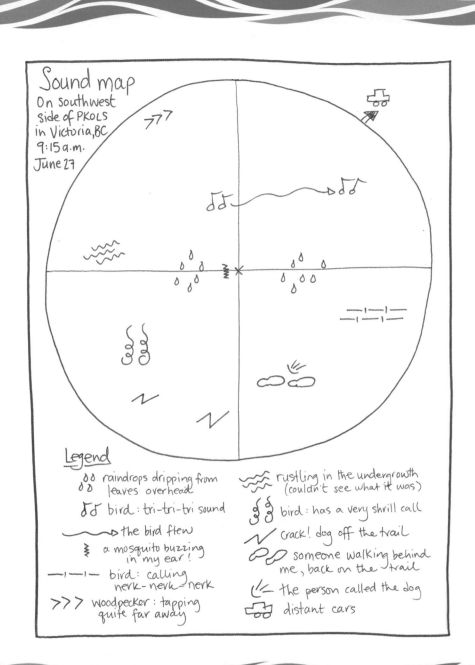

Sound map
On southwest side of PKOLS in Victoria, BC
9:15 a.m.
June 27

Legend

δδ raindrops dripping from leaves overhead

δδ bird: tri-tri-tri sound

⟿ the bird flew

⁑ a mosquito buzzing in my ear!

—ı—ı— bird: calling nerk-nerk-nerk

⟫⟫ woodpecker: tapping quite far away

〜 rustling in the undergrowth (couldn't see what it was)

ξξ bird: has a very shrill call

Ⴌ crack! dog off the trail

∽∽ someone walking behind me, back on the trail

⫭ the person called the dog

🚗 distant cars

author, Hendrik van Loon, had told Howe about "Undersea" and suggested he contact the article's talented but unknown writer.

Van Loon, a well-known historian, journalist, and children's book author and illustrator, also wrote directly to Carson. His quirky, hand-illustrated letter delighted her, but she was also overwhelmed to have attracted the attention of this successful author. A few months later, Carson met with van Loon and Howe to talk about writing a book.

Carson thought hard about how to frame a book about ocean life. She decided to cast different

AUTHORS USING THEIR INITIALS

When Rachel Carson published her essay "Undersea" in the *Atlantic Monthly*, she was identified as R. L. Carson. Many readers assumed the initials stood for a man's name. She explained in a letter to the editor that for this very reason she used her initials for her government writing. As such, she wanted to use her initials for her own writing too.

Many female authors have used initials to make it appear that a man was the author. J. K. Rowling, author of the Harry Potter books, is one. Her publisher worried that boys wouldn't read the book with a female author's name. The J. K. stands for Joanne Kathleen. A few male authors also use initials to make it appear that a woman wrote their book.

Write About an Endangered Animal and Revise Your Essay Using Audio

The "seven-minute fish tales" Rachel Carson wrote for the Bureau of Fisheries were designed to be read aloud on the radio. As she was writing them, Carson might have read her words out loud to hear how they flowed. We know she asked her mother to read out loud from her book manuscripts as she was working on them.

By listening to how your writing sounds you can often hear awkward, repetitive, or confusing words and phrases. You can then change these things during the important phase of writing called editing or revising.

In this activity, you will put your ears to work for your writing.

You'll Need

➤ Pencil and paper, or computer

➤ Library or Internet access

➤ A friend or family member willing to read out loud, or a device to make an audio recording

1. Choose an endangered animal (or plant) to write about. You can find information about endangered species in library books or look online at sites like the IUCN Red List of Threatened Species (www.iucnredlist.org) or the US Fish and Wildlife Service (www.fws.gov/endangered/).

2. Write down a list of basic information about your subject, such as:
   - Common name and scientific name
   - Biome the animal is part of
   - Range (geographic area where it lives)
   - Habitat (abiotic and biotic things the animal likes or needs to survive)
   - Population estimate in the past and present (how many there used to be and when, and how many now exist in the wild)
   - Threats (the things that have made the animal's population go down)
   - Efforts to help the animal (what's being done to increase the population)

3. Make an outline for a three- or four-paragraph essay. For example, your outline could be:
   - Paragraph 1: Introduce the animal and where it lives
   - Paragraph 2: Describe the animal's habitat needs
   - Paragraph 3: Describe threats to the animal and their effects on its population
   - Paragraph 4: Conclude with efforts underway to help the animal

4. Write a first draft of your essay. Remember to use topic sentences and interesting, active vocabulary.

5. Record yourself reading your draft essay and then play back the recording or ask someone to read your essay out loud to you. The first time you listen, don't read along. Just listen. The second time, you can read along and circle words or phrases you want to revise.

6. After you've listened at least twice, revise your essay. You might need to move sentences around, use more descriptive words, or cut out confusing or repetitive parts.

7. Record yourself reading your new draft and then play back the recording or ask someone to read it out loud. Does your essay sound better after revising? Do your words flow more smoothly? Is writing, listening, revising, and re-listening a process you could use for other writing projects?

creatures as her main characters to tell about life from their point of view. She proposed a book in three parts: stories about creatures on the shore, in the open ocean, and in the deep sea. Howe agreed with the general idea, and Carson set to work preparing an outline and writing a chapter.

In spring 1939, Carson sent the first chapter to Howe. He liked it and offered an advance payment of $250, which she accepted. Meanwhile, Carson kept writing articles for the *Baltimore Sun* and continued her day job with the Bureau of Fisheries, which soon merged with another government department and became the Fish and Wildlife Service.

Rachel's Writing Habits

Carson needed total peace to write, so she tended to write in the early morning and late into the evening when the house was quiet. Her cats often

Hendrik van Loon sent Carson a letter in this hand-illustrated envelope in 1937. *By permission of the van Loon family/Rachel Carson Papers, American Literature Collection, Beinecke Rare Book and Manuscript Library, Yale University*

One of Carson's cats attempting to help with her writing. *Rachel Carson Papers, American Literature Collection, Beinecke Rare Book and Manuscript Library, Yale University*

kept her company, helping out in the wonderful way cats do, by sprawling across the pages and notes littering her desk. Carson wrote by hand on sheets of paper and, while she was at work the next day, her mother typed the text. Carson then read the drafts out loud to herself and asked her mother to read them out loud too. Carson revised each sentence again and again until the rhythm of the words on the page pleased her ears as well as her eyes. Then Maria would retype the revised text.

In spring 1940, Carson sent the first part of the book, which told the story of migratory shorebirds called sanderlings, to Howe. He responded with an additional advance of $250 and a deadline for Carson to submit the full book manuscript by the end of the year. The race to write was on.

Carson visited the East Coast again that summer, as she did every summer to either work at Woods Hole or explore another shoreline. All the while, she observed the ocean's creatures and moods, she listened and smelled and felt the whole environment, and she took notes. Sitting at her desk at home again that fall, she wrote, and wrote, and wrote until November, when she completed the entire book manuscript to her satisfaction. Its title was *Under the Sea-Wind: A Naturalist's Picture of Ocean Life.*

Nature's Biomes

Under the Sea-Wind explores a place on Earth called the marine biome. A **biome** is a large ecological area with particular abiotic features and animals adapted to life in that area. Our planet has many biomes: marine, freshwater, forest, grassland, tundra, and desert. Each biome can be separated into several regions or zones that share certain characteristics. On land, the biomes are separated by the types of plants that grow in them. The types of plants depend on temperature and moisture. Plants growing in the warm, wet tropics differ from plants growing in the cold, dry tundra, and differ again from those in hot, dry deserts.

In the marine biome, the zones depend on water depth: the **intertidal** (shore), **nearshore** (shallow depths around the continents), **pelagic** (open water), and **abyssal** (deep sea). In her book, Carson wrote about three of these zones—intertidal, pelagic, and abyssal—and told the life story of a creature for each one. In these stories, Carson described how each creature used its environment to meet its needs. For example, at the beginning of *Under the Sea-Wind*, readers meet two sanderlings (small shorebirds) that Carson referred to as Blackfoot and Silverbar. She described the birds spending the night protected by the sand dunes, and in the morning running in the surf as they hunted for food. Sometimes the waves swept crabs from their sandy burrows, making it easier for Blackfoot and Silverbar to nab a meal. The two sanderlings, along with hundreds of other shorebirds, fed in a frenzy. They all scrambled to eat as much as they could to fuel their long migration north to the Arctic, where they nest and hatch their babies. To fly thousands of miles, sanderlings and other migratory shorebirds need energy, and they get this energy from their environment—the rocky eastern US shores.

Publication Hopes and Woes

When *Under the Sea-Wind* rolled off the printing presses, Carson gave the first copy to her mother, to whom she had dedicated the book. The next copy went to Elmer Higgins with the inscription, "To Mr. Higgins, who started it all." The book appeared on store shelves on November 1, 1941, priced at three dollars.

Now came a test: What kind of reviews would the book receive? And even more importantly to Carson, how would scientists view her writing? To Carson's pleasure, critics at respected publications like the *New York Times Book Review* and the *Christian Science Monitor* wrote favorable reviews.

They noted her poetic writing style and her deep knowledge of ocean life.

Carson was particularly pleased, and probably relieved, that scientists and naturalists also found *Under the Sea-Wind* to be both beautifully and accurately written. With this kind of positive reception in print media and scientific circles, there could have been a rush of people eager to read the book. But, as Carson later said, "The world received the event with superb indifference."

An event that *did* grab the public's attention happened just five weeks after Carson's book was published. On December 7, 1941, Japan bombed Pearl Harbor in Hawaii, and all eyes turned to America's entry into World War II.

Under the Sea-Wind sold fewer than 2,000 copies in 1941 and 1942, leaving Carson deeply disappointed. She blamed world events and criticized her publisher for not doing enough to market the book. Carson decided that in the future she would write only for magazines.

Sanderling feeding on the shore. *iStock.com/ BrianLasenby*

EXPANDING HER RANGE

"My principal hobby is ornithology, in pursuit of which I am always willing to get up in the middle of the night or to get wet, cold, or dirty." —Rachel Carson, writing to the editor of *Outdoor Life*, 1946

When the United States entered World War II in 1941, everyday life changed for millions of people, Rachel Carson included. The government decided to free up office space by moving any department not essential to the war effort away from Washington, DC. The Fisheries department had to move to Chicago.

Carson received this news with dismay, since it meant uprooting her mother and making living arrangements for Virginia and Marjorie, both now finished with high school. One small consolation was that Carson finally received a long-promised promotion to assistant aquatic biologist, along with a salary increase. Her job continued to be primarily writing, reviewing, and editing reports and information sheets. Carson and her mother moved to Chicago in August 1942, but the following spring, they returned to Maryland. Carson had applied for and won a newly vacant job as associate aquatic biologist. Her salary went up again; her duties stayed pretty much the same.

Despite successfully climbing the career ladder, Carson, now 36 years old, was becoming frustrated with her government job. She questioned what her work really meant in the larger context of a world at war. By this time, Carson had also become a respected science writer known for her elegant writing. She thought her writing skills could be valuable and perhaps put to better use if she worked for an organization outside the government. She made a few enquiries about jobs elsewhere, including at *Reader's Digest*, the New York Zoological Society, and the National Audubon Society. There were no openings.

Regardless of any misgivings Carson had about her government job, she continued to do well at it. In 1944 she received two more promotions, first to aquatic biologist and then to information

specialist. Her salary went up and so did her workload. She was now in charge of all the publications put out by the Fisheries department.

Carson also continued to enjoy the friendships she had developed with many of her colleagues. Oftentimes, Ray—as Carson was known at work—and several others would "hide" in her office during their lunch break and use a forbidden hot plate to make tea or coffee. Shirley Briggs, one of Carson's colleagues and friends, told an interviewer years later that Carson was "very bright," "delightful," and "more fun than anybody else."

DDT and the WWII Connection

Carson's government job did have one great advantage: endlessly interesting information came across her desk. During the war, many of the publications she had to edit were about wartime inventions and programs. In this way, she found out about experiments being done by her former boss Elmer Higgins and another government scientist, Clarence Cottam. They were studying fish exposed to a **synthetic chemical** with an impossibly long name: **d**ichloro**d**iphenyl**t**richloroethane, shortened to **DDT**. The military had started using DDT during the war. The chemical was first made in 1873 but at that time it didn't seem to have a use. Years later, in the 1930s, Swiss scientist Paul Hermann Müller discovered its power for killing insects.

During World War II, DDT became the **insecticide** of choice. The military used it to control diseases like malaria and typhus threatening both

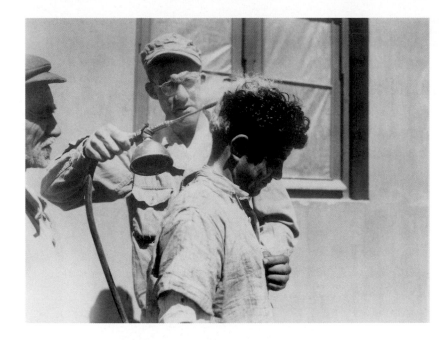

A man is dusted with DDT powder. This photo was taken in 1973. *Gado Images/Alamy Stock Photo*

soldiers and civilians. In 1943 and 1944, in Naples, Italy, infestations of body lice started a typhus epidemic. The lice carried a bacterium that causes typhus, a miserable disease causing high fever, muscle pain, and sometimes even death. Civilians in Naples lined up by the hundreds to receive a dusting of "louse powder"—DDT. Nurses and other members of "dusting squads" received instructions on how to dust people. One scientific article from 1947 noted the instructions, which included "dust the head, pumping the powder against the scalp especially above the back part of the ears" and "the delivery tube is next inserted at the back of the neck and a liberal charge of powder shot down the back." The DDT powder also went under the front of the shirt with special attention to the armpits, down the front and back of a man's trousers, and into a woman's undergarments.

PAUL HERMANN MÜLLER (1899-1965)

In the 1930s, Swiss chemist Paul Hermann Müller was searching for the perfect insecticide. It had to be toxic to insects but not to plants or warm-blooded animals, and it had to be long-lasting. It took him four years of testing different substances before he happened upon one called dichlorodiphenyltrichloroethane, or DDT for short. DDT met all his criteria, or at least, so it seemed in 1939. Müller received the Nobel Prize in Physiology or Medicine in 1948 "for his discovery of the high efficiency of DDT as a contact poison against several arthropods." Over the next 25 years, millions of pounds of DDT were sprayed into the environment all over the world.

Paul Hermann Müller discovered that DDT is a powerful insect poison.
Science History Images/Alamy Stock Photo

This dusting of thousands of people succeeded in squelching Naples's typhus outbreak.

When the war ended in 1945, chemical companies in the United States had warehouses full of DDT. The US Army and the Department of Agriculture agreed that DDT could be sold for public use. It went into all sorts of products: sprays to squirt behind curtains or mist over the picnic table before sitting down to eat, shelf paper to line drawers and cupboards, ready-pasted wallpaper to decorate children's rooms, and flea powders to rub into pet fur. Since DDT seemed harmless, most people used it without hesitation. Only a few scientists suspected that this miracle substance posed a serious threat to wildlife and possibly humans as well.

Higgins and Cottam both wondered whether DDT had unintended effects on wildlife. They started doing experiments at Patuxent Wildlife Research Center in Maryland. Carson was curious and wanted to write an article about their work. In July 1945, she contacted an editor at *Reader's Digest*. "We have all heard a lot about what DDT will soon do for us by wiping out insect pests," she wrote. She went on to say that DDT might also harm beneficial, or helpful, insects like bees, as well as birds that eat insects. Carson suggested an article, but the magazine's editor wasn't interested.

Writing about Bats, Birds, and Lifejackets

Carson shelved the DDT idea for the time being, but she didn't stop writing. She found more ideas in memos that crossed her desk and continued her habit of writing late into the night. Three of the articles she published during the war illustrate an important concept in ecology: by adapting to particular abiotic conditions or features in their environment, organisms can become stronger or more suited to where they live. This concept is sometimes simplified as "**adaptations** give advantages."

In an article titled "Lifesaving Milkweed," Carson wrote about the military's interest in milkweed seedpods as a source of stuffing for life jackets. Before the war, life jackets were stuffed with the buoyant, water-resistant seed fluff from kapok trees grown on Java, an island in Indonesia. When Japan occupied Java during the war, the United States could no longer get the kapok seeds. The fluffy hairs of milkweed seeds made a good substitute, since they're also buoyant and water resistant, as well as warm and lightweight. Milkweed fluff has these qualities because of the plant's way of dispersing, or sending out, seeds into the world. The fluffy seed heads drift like parachutes through the air.

Many plants have evolved seeds that disperse by air: maple trees have seeds with wings like helicopter blades to twirl through the air, jacaranda trees have seeds with papery wings that allow the seed to flutter, and dandelions, like milkweeds, have parachute seeds that drift in a breeze. Seeds that disperse by air can land far from their parent plant, and this gives the plants an advantage: new plants won't compete with existing plants, and the plant population can expand its range.

Carson also wrote about bats, which interested the military because of their ability to fly in the dark. During the war, military airplanes and ships used radar to help them navigate. Radar uses radio waves to detect objects. Carson compared radar with a bat's "method of blind flying," called echolocation. Bats, she wrote, send out "a staccato series of high-pitched cries" that hit an object, bounce back as echoes, and give the bat information to avoid crashing. Echolocation is an adaptation to flying into pitch-dark caves to roost and finding a meal at night, midflight. Carson's article, "The Bat Knew It First," explained radar so clearly that the US Navy used it to help teach recruits about radar technology.

Although some of Carson's writing during the war was inspired by military topics, she had wider interests. She wrote a beautiful manuscript about the chimney swift, a bird that spends most of its life flying. Carson called the swift "a flying insect trap," with its short beak, wide mouth, narrow body, and long wings. These adaptations make swifts especially good at catching insects in the air. Carson also described another of the bird's features: their feet look like hooks. "The swift's idea of going to bed," she wrote, "is merely to hang itself up for the night." This hooked-feet adaptation—useful for roosting in hollow trees—gave swifts an advantage when people cut down trees: the birds started using chimneys instead.

Friends Gained and Lost

As well as spending many hours writing, Carson spent time with friends. She took trips to the seashore and to go bird-watching, a childhood

Create a Seed Bank

All plants and animals have needs—a home, food, and so on—that must be met by the environment they live in. To become better suited to their environment, plants and animals adapt, or gradually change in their appearance, function, or behavior. Different organisms adapt in different ways depending on their needs and environment.

Seeds are a wonderful example of how different plants have adapted in different ways. Most plants reproduce by making seeds. The seeds disperse, or get taken away from the parent plant, and germinate to grow a new generation of plants. Seeds can be dispersed in many ways, and they have unique features to help with dispersal, as shown in the chart below.

You'll Need

➤ Backyard or a park (best in mid- to late summer or in fall when many plants have set seed)

➤ 6–10 small plastic snack bags

➤ Clear tape

➤ Permanent marker or sticky labels

➤ Paper and pencil

➤ Paper towel

➤ Poster board

1. Collect a variety of seeds from plants in your yard or local park. Depending on the time of year and your region, you may find dandelion seeds, grass heads, burrs, rose hips, maple keys, peapods, cotton-wood fluff, coconuts, berries—the list

Dispersal Method	Common Features Seed Might Have (not necessarily all of them)	Plants That Use This Dispersal Method
Wind	• Lightweight • Wings or blades • Fluffy or feathery • Parachute-like	Dandelion, sycamore tree, maple tree
Water	• Waterproof coating or shell • Able to float	Coconut palm, water lily
Explosion (bursting out of seed head)	• Small • Many seeds from single seed head	Poppy, pea, witch hazel
Food for animals	• Large and heavy • Inside a nutritious, fleshy fruit • Bright colors	Blackberry, mango, oak tree
Hitchhiker on animals	• Hooks, barbs, or small spikes • Sticky	Hedge parsley, sandbur (a grass)
Fire	• Able to stay dormant for a long time • Inside cones that open only at high temperature from fire	lodgepole pine, eucalyptus

is endless. Try to collect 6–10 types of seeds with different shapes and features.

2. Place a few of each seed into a plastic bag, with one bag for each type of plant. (If the bags are too big, cut them and reseal the edges with tape.) Using the permanent marker or a sticky label, label each bag with the name or a description of the plant the seed came from.

3. Draw a chart, like the one below, on a piece of paper. Examine each type of seed you collected and fill in the chart. One row is completed, for a dandelion seed, to help you get started.

4. Compare the seeds you found. Do ones with the same way of dispersing have similar characteristics?

5. When you have finished the chart, lay a few specimens of each seed on a paper towel and leave them in an airy spot to dry. Some will dry quickly (or may not even need to dry, like ripe poppy seeds), and others like tomato seeds may take several days.

6. When they're dry, return the seeds to their labeled plastic bags and tape them onto a poster board for display.

Name or Description of Parent Plant	Sketch of Seed	Features of Seed	Possible Reasons for Seed's Features	How the Seed Might Be Dispersed (given its features)
Dandelion		— Lightweight — Feathery tuft — Pointy at end	— Lightweight for easy wind transport — Tuft allows wind to carry it — Pointy end heavier than tuft to settle into soil when it lands — Pointy end might attach to animal fur	— By the wind — On animal fur

Optional: If you want to try planting the seeds in the future, keep them in a cool, dark place instead of on a poster board. This will increase the chances of their successful germination.

TWO BAGS, ONE LIFE

Milkweed is considered by many to be a nuisance plant. It tends to grow in ditches along roadsides and fields. You might know it as a critical plant for monarch butterflies, since it's the only one they will lay their eggs on. During World War II, children were asked to help the war effort by collecting ripe milkweed pods in the fall. An article in a Missouri newspaper reported that pod pickers would be paid 20 cents for each onion bag of dried milkweed pods. It also said "a satisfactorily filled bag should contain about 800 pods" and that "the floss in two bags of milkweed pods fills a life jacket, so a collection, even though it is small, may help save a life."

Schoolchildren pointing at the bags of milkweed pods they've collected for the war effort in 1944. *Courtesy of the McLean County Museum of History, Bloomington, Illinois*

Floss from ripe milkweed pods. *iStock.com/chas53*

passion that never left her. When she was younger, she had started a list of the birds she saw, and she kept adding to it throughout her life.

One of her favorite locations for bird-watching was Hawk Mountain Sanctuary in Pennsylvania. There, Carson and her work friend Shirley Briggs climbed to the tip of craggy peaks to peer skyward through binoculars. Among the birds they might have spotted are American kestrels, turkey vultures, red-tailed hawks, and bald eagles. Even on Hawk Mountain, about 100 miles from the coast, Carson kept the ocean in her thoughts, writing in her field notebook about the streams tumbling down the mountains and ultimately flowing out to the sea.

Katherine Howe, or Kay, was another of Carson's friends from work. Kay and Shirley were illustrators hired by the Bureau of Commercial Fisheries. Both women were younger than Carson by about a decade, but the three of them formed a tight friendship. In 1946, Carson led a new project, joined by Howe and Briggs, to publish 12 booklets about national wildlife refuges in a series titled Conservation in Action. Its purpose was to tell the public about threats to wildlife and efforts needed to preserve wildlife in the United States. The research for these booklets took Carson, Briggs, and Howe on field trips across the country.

In April, Carson and Briggs traveled to Virginia to learn more about the Chincoteague refuge, where waterfowl and shorebirds stop to refuel on their long migrations. In interviews with a Carson biographer many years later, Briggs described how she and Carson tramped morning and evening through the lobby of their hotel. The sight of these strange characters wearing wet, muddy garments and lugging assorted gear—cameras, binoculars, and so on—startled the other hotel guests.

For a month in the fall, Carson and Howe traveled by train to visit refuges in Utah and Montana, as well as fish hatcheries along Oregon's portion

Carson bird-watching at Hawk Mountain Sanctuary, Pennsylvania.
Shirley A. Briggs/By permission of Rachel Carson Council, Inc.

Invent a Creature and Its Ecosystem

One of the basic concepts in ecology is that animals and plants adapt to their environment. Adaptation to different conditions explains why planet Earth has so much biological diversity, or biodiversity.

In this activity, you will create an ecosystem and invent a creature adapted to life in that ecosystem.

You'll Need

➤ Empty shoebox

➤ Craft materials (colored papers, pipe cleaners, feathers, pom-poms, popsicle sticks)

➤ Found outdoor objects (twigs, leaves, pebbles, tree cones, shells)

➤ Small indoor items (buttons, dental floss, paper clips, hair elastics)

➤ Craft glue, glue stick, or clear tape

➤ Scissors

➤ Markers

➤ Paper and pencil

➤ Modeling clay

1. Turn the shoebox on its side and use the craft materials, found objects, and small items to create an ecosystem. It can look as little or as much like a real ecosystem as you choose. As you design and build your ecosystem, think about what sort of temperature, light, and weather it might have, as well as what kinds of shelter, food, water, and predators it might contain.

2. Write one or two sentences describing the environment you've chosen, especially the features that might be hard to show, like temperature.

3. Use the modeling clay to create a creature that lives in your ecosystem. It can look as little or as much like a real animal as you choose. Think about how it looks, how it moves, where and how it sleeps, what it eats, and how it gets its food. The creature's characteristics should relate in some way to features of your ecosystem.

4. Give your creature a name that fits its appearance or way of living.

5. Place your creature in the ecosystem and explain to a friend, family member, or teacher how it is adapted to live in its ecosystem.

NATIONAL WILDLIFE REFUGE SYSTEM

"If you travel much in the wilder sections of our country, sooner or later you are likely to meet the sign of the flying goose—the emblem of the National Wildlife Refuges. . . . Wild creatures, like men, must have a place to live. As civilization creates cities, builds highways, and drains marshes, it takes away, little by little, the land that is suitable for wildlife. And as their space for living dwindles, the wildlife populations themselves decline. Refuges resist this trend."

—Rachel Carson, introduction to "Chincoteague: A National Wildlife Refuge," first booklet of the Conservation in Action series, 1947

The National Wildlife Refuge System began in 1903 when Pelican Island in Florida was set aside in an effort to save brown pelicans. There are now more than 560 refuges across the country.

A refuge established on the coast of Maine in 1966 was rededicated four years later as the Rachel Carson National Wildlife Refuge. It protects forests, beaches, sand dunes, meadows, tidal salt marshes, and rocky coast for hundreds of bird species, many of them migratory birds. These habitats are also home to a host of animals, from white-tailed deer and river otters to painted turtles and tree frogs.

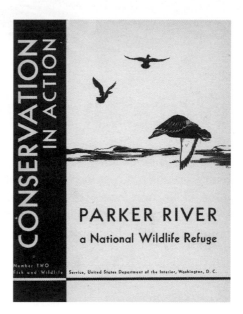

The front cover of one of the Conservation in Action booklets written by Carson and illustrated by Kay Howe. *US Fish and Wildlife Service*

of the Columbia River. On this trip, Carson and Howe spent a day at a beach along the Oregon coast where, for the first time, Carson set eyes on the Pacific Ocean.

Much as Carson enjoyed the traveling and writing for the Conservation in Action booklets, she still wished that she could dedicate more time to her own writing. Her government job came with the demands of managing a staff of six people to deliver Fish and Wildlife's publication program.

On the home front, Carson's mother had to have surgery, and Carson herself wound up as a patient in hospital not once, nor twice, but three times in a span of under two years. As if this weren't enough, in early 1948, Carson suffered a bad case of shingles. Shingles is a viral

Write an Animal's Résumé

A *résumé* is something you will write when you're looking for a job. It tells an employer about your education, work experience, skills, and interests. Typically, a résumé has sections for your basic information (name, contact, etc.), career or job goal, education, work or volunteer experience, skills, and interests or hobbies.

In this activity, you will practice formatting and writing a résumé by preparing one for an animal. The sections will be a little different for an animal résumé—basic information, background, behaviors, adaptations, interests—but the format is the same.

You'll Need

➤ Pencil and paper, or computer

➤ Library or Internet access

1. Choose an animal that interests you and research its appearance, behavior, habitat, and adaptations to its habitat. Use library books or websites like www.nationalgeographic.com/animals, www.canadiangeographic.ca/kids, www.worldwildlife.org/species, and www.allaboutbirds.org. Take notes as you do your research.

2. Use this polar bear example as a guide to write a résumé for the animal you chose. Be sure to format the résumé to look professional and appealing.

EXAMPLE RÉSUMÉ

Name: Polar bear, *Ursus maritimus*
Habitat: Sea ice, High Arctic
Size: 800–1,300 pounds, 6–9 feet long
Life span: About 25 years
Life goals: To hunt for food, preferably seals. For a male, to father cubs. For a female, to have and raise cubs.

Background:
• Member of mammal class
• Earth's only marine bear
• Largest carnivore in North America

continued on next page . . .

Behaviors:
- Cleaning fur and paws by swimming and then shaking off or by rolling in snow
- Grooming paws to get ice chunks out
- Greeting another bear nose to nose
- Play fighting
- Digging shallow snow pits to sleep in

Adaptations:
- White coat to camouflage in snow and ice
- Thick outer fur with special hairs to repel water
- Dense layer of underfur, black skin, and thick layer of fat to keep warm
- Small ears and short tail to lose as little heat as possible
- Strong paws with sharp claws to hunt with
- Bumpy foot pads to avoid slipping on ice
- Good sense of smell to find seals
- Ability to slow down metabolism (internal body functions) to save energy when haven't eaten for many days
- Large front paws to use as paddles when swimming

Interests:
- Hunting
- Sleeping
- Swimming
- Being alone a lot of the time
- Raising cubs and teaching them how to survive in the Arctic (female bears)

infection—from the same virus that causes chicken pox—and gives people an excruciatingly painful rash.

Despite these episodes of poor health, Carson kept reading and thinking about the ocean. She had been collecting information about the science of the sea for years. She sifted through her notes and tossed ideas around in her mind. Her thoughts turned to writing another book about the ocean, a book describing its origins, geography, physics, chemistry, and biology.

At the urging of a friend, Carson finally agreed that she needed help managing her writing career. She interviewed several literary agents and decided to sign on as a client with Marie Rodell, a writer and editor who had just formed her own literary agency. By agreeing to work together, Carson and Rodell began a partnership and friendship that lasted for the rest of Carson's life.

A few months later, in November 1948, Carson received a call telling her that her friend Mary Skinker was gravely ill with cancer and wanted to be in touch with her. Carson flew to Chicago to be by Skinker's side. Mary Skinker died a few weeks later, just 57 years old. The woman who had sparked Carson's interest in studying biology, and particularly the ocean, was gone. Carson felt her loss deeply.

5

UNDER THE SEA AND ON TOP OF THE WORLD

"These deep, dark waters, with all their mysteries and their unsolved problems, cover a very considerable part of the earth." —Rachel Carson, *The Sea Around Us*, 1951

Step by step, Rachel Carson went backward down a ladder into the waters of Biscayne Bay, off the coast of Florida. She had an 84-pound diving helmet over her head. She climbed down until she stood on the seafloor beneath the dive boat. Carson saw sea fans, corals, and some colorful fish, but little else since bad weather had churned up the seabed, making the water murky. She felt the pull of the water currents as she gripped the ladder.

Carson sitting in a dive boat with a cumbersome diving helmet at her feet, 1949. *Shirley Briggs/Courtesy of Linda Lear Center for Special Collections and Archives, Connecticut College*

Though brief and seemingly not very exciting, this single trip into the ocean made a huge impression on Carson. For years she had been wanting to go beneath the surface to witness the underwater world firsthand. And now, she had. Afterward, she told her friend William Beebe, a well-known scientist and deep-sea explorer, that her dive had been the kind of experience that changes a person's outlook on the world.

Away at Sea

Right after the Florida trip, Carson went off on another ocean adventure with her agent, Marie

---

WILLIAM BEEBE (1877–1962)

William Beebe had an avid curiosity about the natural world. He worked for the New York Zoological Park (now the Bronx Zoo) as curator, or keeper, of birds and later as director of its Department of Tropical Research. He went on expeditions to study birds and wildlife all over the world and wrote articles and books about his many adventures.

In the 1920s, Beebe began helmet diving, and he wondered about diving to the deep sea with some kind of diving vessel. Nobody had ever traveled down to see deep-sea creatures in their habitats. Beebe met Otis Barton, an engineer who was also interested in the idea of deep-sea diving. Barton had designed a spherical diving vessel with portholes to look through and a cable to suspend it from a boat. Beebe and Barton agreed to work together to build the diving vessel, which they called a "bathysphere." They then tested it, making many dives together sealed inside the cramped sphere. In 1934, they descended into the waters off Bermuda to their record depth of 3,028 feet.

Beebe wrote a complimentary review of Carson's first book, *Under the Sea-Wind*, and later included two of her chapters in a collection of natural history essays published as *The Book of Naturalists: An Anthology of the Best Natural History*. Carson and Beebe corresponded by letter and later they met. It was Beebe who encouraged Carson to experience the undersea world by going on a diving expedition.

Otis Barton and William Beebe with their bathysphere, 1934.
Sueddeutsche Zeitung Photo/Alamy Stock Photo

Rodell. They traveled aboard a government research boat called the *Albatross III* that was headed for Georges Bank off the northeast coast of the United States.

Georges Bank is an area of shallow water where the cold Labrador current brings nutrient-rich water to meet warmer Gulf Stream currents. The mixing of these two water currents, plus sunlight, makes perfect conditions for tiny **algae** to grow in the water. These tiny algae are called **phytoplankton**. "Phyto" means *plant* and "**plankton**" means *drifting*, so the phytoplankton are drifting plants. They use sunlight to fuel photosynthesis, and nutrients from the water to grow and multiply. The many phytoplankton become food for small drifting animals—the **zooplankton**. And the zooplankton are food for fish. This is a simple **food chain**.

Ecologists study food chains in ecosystems throughout the world, not just in the ocean. The different players in a food chain are labeled according to their role. At the bottom are the **producers** (phytoplankton in the ocean, plants on land), next come **primary consumers** (zooplankton in the ocean, **herbivores** like grasshoppers, deer, and mice on land), and then **secondary consumers** (**planktivores** like certain fish and whales in the ocean, **carnivores** like cougars, foxes, and eagles on land).

Some food chains have **tertiary** and even **quaternary consumers** too. Each layer in a chain is called a **trophic level** and tells how many feeding layers exist between a producer and a consumer. Producers are always the first trophic level, and each consumer layer then adds on to make a second trophic level, a third trophic level, and so on.

One other player in an ecosystem is the **decomposer**. Decomposers are organisms like bacteria, fungi, and some animals like worms, snails, and certain insects. Decomposers don't really occupy a trophic level, but they do have an important job in recycling dead plants and animals.

When several food chains mingle and intertwine with each other, they make a network called a **food web**. The reality of ecosystems is that many different feeding relationships can be happening all at once, so food webs tend to be untidy things when biologists draw them on paper.

Carson wrote many times about food chains, food webs, and the dance—or battle—of eating and being eaten. Some of her most beautiful passages appear in her first book, *Under the Sea-Wind*. In one scene, Carson wrote about Scomber, a mackerel fish that has recently hatched from its egg and is learning what to eat. Soon, Scomber very nearly meets his end:

Out of the clear green water a dozen gleaming silver fishes suddenly loomed up. They were anchovies, small and herringlike. The foremost anchovy caught sight of Scomber. Swerving from his path, he came whirling through the yard of water that separated them, open-mouthed, ready to seize the small mackerel. Scomber veered away in sudden alarm, but his powers of motion were new-found and he rolled clumsily in the water. In a fraction of a second he would have been seized and eaten, but a second anchovy, darting in from the opposite side, collided with the first and in the confusion Scomber dashed beneath them.

As the action continues, the anchovies themselves meet danger when a school of bluefish start attacking them, "fierce and ravening as a pack of wolves." Scomber escapes unharmed.

Carson's trip aboard the *Albatross III* in July 1949 allowed her to gather firsthand information to write about the Fish and Wildlife Service's work in conserving the Georges Bank fishing grounds. More than a hundred different species of fish, including cod, haddock, and flounder, live there. Many of these fish are (or used to be) valuable for commercial fisheries.

Carson and her agent, Marie Rodell, spent 10 days aboard the *Albatross III* research vessel, shown here leaving the dock at Woods Hole, Massachusetts.
© Woods Hole Oceanographic Institution

The 10-day trip also gave Carson a chance to experience the open ocean with its wind and fog and choppy waves. She got to see several oceanographic instruments collecting data. One recorded water temperature, and another traced the floor of the seabed, showing how the level floor suddenly dropped steeply as the ship passed over deep undersea canyons. She examined the contents of dredging nets that hauled creatures—starfish, urchins, crabs, sponges, and many types of fish—from deep in the ocean up to the ship's deck.

Carson returned home filled with excitement about her next book project. Putting aside her earlier misgivings, she had decided to write a book about the ocean. Rodell had encouraged her and found a willing publisher. Earlier in the summer, Carson had signed a contract with Oxford University Press and written several chapters of a book with the title *Return to the Sea*. Now, as she dove back into her writing, she drew upon the sights, sounds, smells, and feelings she had experienced on the *Albatross III* adventure, as well as her journey beneath the waves in Florida.

The Writer at Work

Carson was thrilled to receive a grant that summer, called the Saxton Fellowship, which awarded money to promising writers. The grant meant Carson could take off the month of October from her job to focus on writing her ocean book.

As always, Carson's mother, Maria, helped her daughter by typing draft after draft of the manuscript. Carson wrote slowly and revised her words time and again. She didn't get as much done as she'd hoped during the month off because Marjorie, the younger of her two nieces, became ill and Carson looked after her.

As 1949 gave way to 1950, Carson kept writing the many different chapters, including ones about tides, currents, waves, islands, and shorelines. Oftentimes, the writing seemed more like struggling, but slowly she got through each chapter and sent it to scientists to comment on what she'd written. For Carson, scientific accuracy was as important as graceful writing.

As the manuscript began to take shape, Carson and Rodell discussed the book's title. Neither of them liked *Return to the Sea*, but none of their

Carson working at her microscope. *Brooks Studio/Rachel Carson Papers, American Literature Collection, Beinecke Rare Book and Manuscript Library, Yale University*

THE CALAMITOUS COD COLLAPSE

For centuries, people have fished for cod, halibut, haddock, lobster, and many other species on the Grand Banks and Georges Bank. These shallow areas lie off the coasts of Newfoundland, Nova Scotia, Maine, and Massachusetts. The ocean conditions there—temperature, light, nutrients—make for abundant phytoplankton and zooplankton, and in turn many fish.

Beginning in the late 1400s, productive fisheries in this area fed people in Europe, and later in North America and the Caribbean. By the 1900s, fishing boats and gear had begun to change from small boats with fishing lines and baited hooks to trawlers. These larger boats with long dragnets and powerful winches could scoop many more fish from the ocean. After World War II, commercial fishing soared to new heights—literally. Airplanes with sonar detected schools of fish, and enormous factory ships then hauled in as much as they could catch.

Alarmed by the fishing pressure from international fleets, the United States banned foreign boats from Georges Bank. Canada did the same for the Grand Banks. Even so, by the early 1990s the cod population had collapsed from overfishing. Canada closed its commercial cod fishery in 1993, and the fishery is still shut today. Soon after Canada's ban, the United States stopped fishing on parts of Georges Bank and placed tight restrictions on other areas. Scientists think the Atlantic cod population seems to be coming back, but very slowly.

Examine Food Chains and Food Webs

Many of the articles Rachel Carson wrote in the early years of her publishing career were about fish and other creatures in Chesapeake Bay. Below is one of the bay's simple food chains. The arrows show the feeding relationship from food to eater. In this food chain, diatoms (phytoplankton) are food for copepods (zooplankton), which are food for menhaden (small fish), which are food for herons (large birds).

In this activity, you'll take a closer look at food chains and webs using residents of Chesapeake Bay.

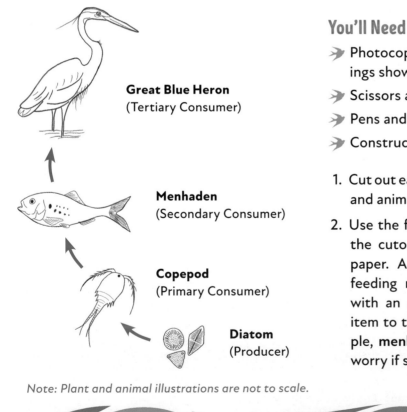

Great Blue Heron
(Tertiary Consumer)

Menhaden
(Secondary Consumer)

Copepod
(Primary Consumer)

Diatom
(Producer)

Note: Plant and animal illustrations are not to scale.

You'll Need

➤ Photocopy of the plant and animal drawings shown on page 55

➤ Scissors and clear tape

➤ Pens and colored pencils or markers

➤ Construction paper

1. Cut out each of the Chesapeake Bay plants and animals on your copy of page 55.

2. Use the following 10 statements to place the cutouts on a sheet of construction paper. Arrange the organisms to show feeding relationships by drawing a line with an arrow pointing from each food item to the eater of that item. For example, **menhaden ⟶ striped bass**. Don't worry if some lines cross over others.

a. Diatoms and wild celery use sunlight for photosynthesis.

b. Copepods eat diatoms.

c. Clams filter diatoms from the water.

d. Canvasback eat wild celery and clams.

e. Menhaden eat copepods.

f. Terns eat menhaden and clams.

g. Striped bass eat menhaden.

h. Osprey eat menhaden and striped bass.

i. Bald eagles eat canvasback, menhaden, and striped bass.

j. Great blue herons eat menhaden and terns.

5. In the food web you've created, find the simple food chain shown in the introduction to this activity. Draw a rectangle around it. What's different between this food chain and the food web? Can you find two more simple food chains within this food web?

6. Use a green pencil or marker to circle all the producers. Use blue to circle all the primary consumers, yellow for secondary consumers, orange for tertiary consumers, and red for quaternary consumers. Some animals will get more than one colored circle. What do the colors tell you about the food web? How many trophic levels are in this food web?

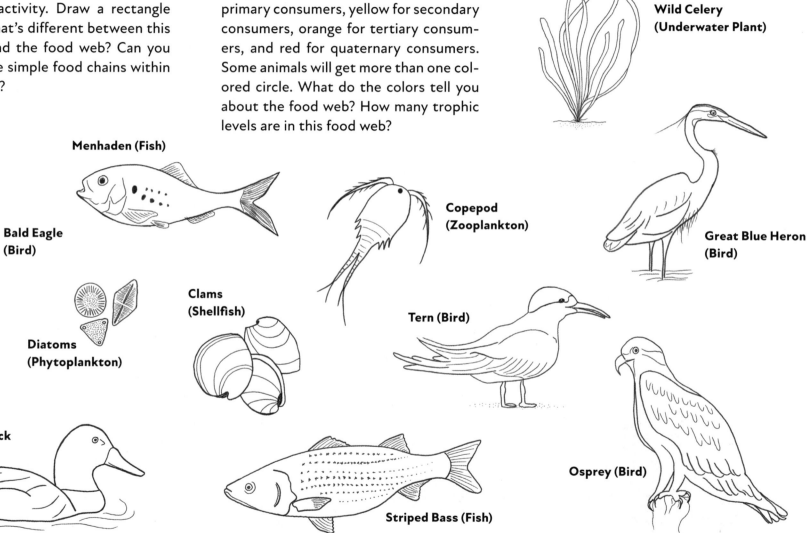

Wild Celery (Underwater Plant)

Menhaden (Fish)

Bald Eagle (Bird)

Copepod (Zooplankton)

Great Blue Heron (Bird)

Diatoms (Phytoplankton)

Clams (Shellfish)

Tern (Bird)

Canvasback (Bird)

Striped Bass (Fish)

Osprey (Bird)

other ideas seemed quite right either. They toyed with titles like *The Story of the Ocean* and *Sea Without End*. A few of Carson's friends joked about her title troubles, offering cheeky suggestions like *Out of My Depth* and *Carson at Sea*.

Eventually, Carson and the editor at Oxford University Press settled on a title, and by June 1950, Carson had finished the manuscript of her second book: *The Sea Around Us*. As well as getting the publishing contract, Rodell had arranged for the *New Yorker* magazine to buy nine of the book's chapters and publish short versions of them before the book appeared in print. Carson earned more from those nine chapters than a year's salary at her government job!

After delivering her manuscript, Carson had to wait. She fretted that the American military involvement in Korea might stifle her new book's success, much like Pearl Harbor had done to *Under the Sea-Wind*.

During her wait, Carson discovered a lump in her breast. The doctor who removed it told her all was well. Carson believed him and dismissed Rodell's concerns. Besides, Carson had other projects on the go, including a guidebook to the seashore that an editor at Houghton Mifflin, another book publishing company, had asked her to write.

Runaway Bestseller

Finally, in June 1951, the first installment of *The Sea Around Us* came out in the *New Yorker*. Fan mail poured into the magazine's office, with readers praising Carson's poetic writing. On July 2, when the book itself appeared on bookstore shelves, readers clamored to buy copies.

Carson was unprepared for the flood of attention. She couldn't understand why newspapers and magazines wanted to print her photo and write about her. She thought they should be focusing on the book. Some of the readers and reviewers of *The Sea Around Us* found it necessary to comment that a book about the ocean had been written by a woman. In a speech years later, Carson described receiving letters with such statements as, "I assume from the author's knowledge that he must be a man." Another comment, spoken directly to her was, "I thought you would be a very large and forbidding woman."

Apart from the attention on her appearance and gender, Carson was thankful that her second book hadn't been ignored like her first. She was also thrilled that the scientists who commented on her book generally admired the way she explained the science of the ocean.

Carson received calls too. One came from former President Theodore Roosevelt's daughter, Alice Roosevelt Longworth, who phoned early one morning to say that she'd stayed up all night reading *The Sea Around Us*. Rodell also fielded phone calls with requests for interviews, speeches, and articles. Carson declined many of the requests, but she accepted some. She agreed to write the jacket notes for a vinyl record of the NBC Symphony Orchestra playing *La Mer* (French for *The Ocean*), composed by Claude Debussy. Carson didn't play an instrument, but she had grown up listening to her mother's piano students and she loved classical

Carson's portrait taken for the release of *The Sea Around Us*. *Brooks Studio/By permission of Rachel Carson Council, Inc.*

music. In the jacket notes for *La Mer*, she wrote about waves, saying, "As they roll majestically in open ocean or as they break and surge at the edge of land, their voices are the voice of the sea."

Three weeks after publication, *The Sea Around Us* made it onto the *New York Times* bestseller list at number five. It then climbed up the list, and by September it sat at number one, where it stayed right into April 1952. In all, the book remained on this bestseller list for 86 weeks.

With all this success and book sales approaching 100,000 copies, the publisher rereleased Carson's first book, *Under the Sea-Wind*. This book also made it onto the *New York Times* bestseller list, and for a while, both of Carson's books were listed at the same time. Carson received other compliments too. She was given honorary degrees and many awards, including the John Burroughs Medal for best book of nature writing and the National Book Award for nonfiction.

Sudden Fame and Fortune

For many of the awards, Carson had to give an acceptance speech. She learned to become a good public speaker but never relished the spotlight. She was a private person who most enjoyed spending time quietly in nature and libraries, and with her family, friends, and cats. As much as possible, she tried to escape the attention shining on her.

Carson's mother, Maria, by now 83 years old, also got drawn into the frenzy swirling around

Alice Roosevelt Longworth and Carson reading her book together at the National Book Award ceremonies.
Rachel Carson Papers, American Literature Collection, Beinecke Rare Book and Manuscript Library, Yale University

Carson and her book. Maria helped by replying to the fan mail, answering the telephone, and intercepting many of the requests that came to their home. When Carson escaped to Woods Hole to do some research, Maria stayed at home and kept up with the deluge as best she could.

Much as Carson struggled with the unexpected celebrity status she had gained as the author of a runaway bestseller, she understood it in practical terms. For the first time ever, she didn't have to worry about how to pay the rent or grocery bill. Carson now had money to spare.

Make a Food Pyramid

Feeling hungry is your body's way of warning that you need more energy. You eat a snack; you're a consumer.

All consumers in ecosystems are the same: they eat to get energy to live and grow. If a consumer gets eaten by a predator (also a consumer), the predator gets energy. In this way, energy flows from one step—one trophic level—of the food chain to the next.

It also takes energy to find, eat, and digest food, so the energy that goes to these activities isn't available to consumers in the next trophic level. Therefore, each higher trophic level has fewer animals in total than the last.

Ecologists represent the flow of energy in ecosystems using pyramids. The base represents the most abundant organisms, the producers. The next layer represents the primary consumers. Each layer—each trophic level—is smaller than the previous one because it has fewer animals. The tip of the pyramid represents the highest trophic level.

You can picture this flow of energy by constructing a food pyramid. Below is a diagram of one food chain in a desert ecosystem. Each arrow shows the feeding relationship from a food item to a consumer. In this food chain, cactuses are food for rats, which are food for rattlesnakes, which are food for hawks.

Red-Tailed Hawk
(Tertiary Consumer)

Diamondback Rattlesnake
(Secondary Consumer)

Prickly Pear Cactus
(Producer)

Wood Rat
(Primary Consumer)

Note: Plant and animal illustrations are not to scale.

You'll Need

➤ Photocopy of the food pyramid
➤ Scissors
➤ Clear tape, craft glue, or glue stick
➤ Pens and colored pencils or markers

1. Write the word at the top of each of these columns in the smallest spaces of the pyramid, then use the second word down in each column to fill the next smallest set of spaces in the pyramid. Continue in this way with the third and fourth sets of words:

- tertiary consumer
- secondary consumer
- primary consumer
- producer

- red-tailed hawk
- diamondback rattlesnake
- wood rat
- prickly pear cactus

- carnivore
- carnivore
- herbivore
- producer

2. Cut on all the dotted lines and then fold and tape or glue the paper into a pyramid shape.

3. What would happen at each step of the food chain if a pesticide made the eggshells of red-tailed hawks so thin that they broke before the chicks could hatch?

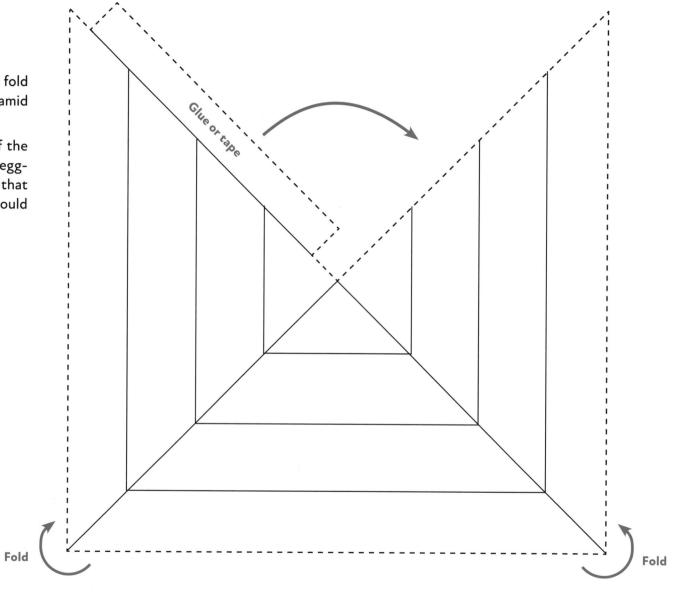

Glue or tape

Fold

Fold

Go on an Ecosystem Scavenger Hunt

Maria and Rachel Carson were both keen explorers of nature, spending a lot of Rachel's childhood together outside. The observation skills she learned during these years became the foundation of how she learned about ecosystems for the rest of her life.

One way to heighten your observation skills is to go on a nature walk with a list of things to find: leaves, tree cones, seashells, and so on. In this activity, the scavenger hunt steps up a notch with some of the things you've learned about ecosystems.

You'll Need

- Comfortable clothing
- Photocopy of the list of items to find
- Pencil
- Notebook (or other hard surface to lean on as you write)

Go for a walk in a park or other natural area—a forest, a beach, a meadow, along a river. Tick off as many of the items on the list as you can and make notes on your paper.

ECOSYSTEM SCAVENGER HUNT FORM

The ecosystem I'm exploring is _____. It is part of the _____ biome.

❑ ❑ ❑ Three non-living (abiotic) parts of the ecosystem. What are they? _____

_____

❑ ❑ ❑ Three living (biotic) parts of the ecosystem. What are they? _____

_____

❑ An interaction between something biotic and something abiotic. What are the two things and what is the interaction between them? _____

_____

_____

❑ A source of water for an organism in the ecosystem _____

_____

❏ An insect's home. What does it look like? Can you identify the insect that lives there? _____
_____

❏ Evidence of a decomposer. What is the evidence? Can you identify the decomposer from the evidence? _____
_____

❏ Evidence of a consumer. What is the evidence? Can you identify the consumer from the evidence? _____
_____

❏ A producer. What is it? _____

❏ A primary consumer. What is it? _____

❏ A secondary consumer. What is it? _____

❏ A tertiary consumer that might live in or visit the ecosystem. What is it? _____
_____

❏ An example of erosion. What is it, and what do you think caused it? _____
_____

❏ What biotic and abiotic things might be affected by the erosion you found above? _____
_____

❏ ❏ Two plants with different adaptations. What are the plants, and what are their adaptations? _____
_____

❏ ❏ Two animals with different adaptations. What are the animals, and what are their adaptations? _____
_____

THE WONDER OF NATURE

"Those who contemplate the beauty of the earth find reserves of strength that will endure as long as life lasts." —Rachel Carson, *The Sense of Wonder*, 1965

A seagull squawks as it soars overhead. The water sparkles and laps gently against seaweed-covered rocks. Below and among the weed sit snail shells of all sizes and colors, some occupied, others abandoned. The scent of salty water and drying seaweed drifts in the air.

This is the low-tide zone of a stretch of rocky shore on Southport Island in Maine. Beyond the ocean's reach and up a shrub-covered cliff stands a forest. Pine and spruce

The shore in front of Carson's cottage on Southport Island. *Rowena Rae* trees filter the sunlight that dapples the floor below. A red squirrel scampers up a tree trunk; a hermit thrush warbles unseen. This shore and these woods offer tranquility to anyone who cares to pause and breathe in their beauty.

Rachel Carson decided to buy a piece of property on Southport Island—140 feet along the shoreline and 350 feet up into the forest. Especially appealing were the tide pools where she could explore for hours. In 1952, when Carson fell in love with this patch of Southport Island, she was already hard at work on her next book. The book was to be a guide to the seashore, so Carson was excited at the prospect of having her own piece of shore to search for organisms.

Isolation was another appealing aspect of the Southport Island property. With all the hubbub following *The Sea Around Us*, Carson relished a place of her own where she could retreat from the limelight and enjoy the privacy she cherished. With the money she earned on sales of *The Sea Around Us*, Carson could afford not only to buy a piece of land but also to have a cottage built on it.

Carson had another reason for wanting to safeguard her and her family's privacy. Only a few months after *The Sea Around Us* hit the bestseller lists, Carson's younger niece confided in her. Marjorie was pregnant. Not only was she unmarried, but the baby's father was already married to someone else. In the 1950s, having a baby "out of wedlock," as it was termed, brought social disgrace upon the mother and her family. For Carson, just as her long-desired writing career had begun to soar, family worries once again intruded.

Besides fearing scandal, Carson and her mother worried about Marjorie and her health. Marjorie had diabetes, a disease that can bring many complications with it. Pregnancy is hard enough on a healthy woman's body, so for a woman with diabetes, pregnancy comes with added risks. Carson made sure that Marjorie got good medical care, but even so, she ended up in hospital several times before her baby boy—Roger—was born on February 18, 1952.

Full-Time Writer

In June 1951, Carson began a one-year leave of absence. This meant that she wouldn't work for or be paid by her employer for 12 months, but her job would be saved for her. When the year was over, Carson could have picked up where she left off, but she didn't. With her book's success and with freedom from money worries, she decided to resign from her government job. In June 1952, she became an independent, full-time writer!

Carson now had more time to write, but she felt pulled in multiple directions all at once. On the writing side, she had her seashore book partway written. She also had a contract with a filmmaker who wanted to shoot a documentary version of *The Sea Around Us*. On the personal side, she had an aging mother, a niece with health problems and a baby, and a cottage under construction in Maine.

With so much going on, Carson struggled to focus on writing. The original idea for the seashore book had come from Paul Brooks, editor in chief at Houghton Mifflin, another publishing company. Brooks was to become both a trusted editor and a friend.

Carson was trying to write the book, but it just wasn't working. It felt disjointed and no different from any other guide to seashore life. She struggled for many months before taking a trip to Florida and hitting on a solution. Instead of writing short descriptions of one creature after another, she would write about the three major types of shore along the Atlantic coastline. The rocky shores north of Cape Cod experienced incoming and outgoing tides that influenced the ecology. From the mid-Atlantic to Florida, waves crashed on the sandy shores dictating the types of creatures that could survive. And the Florida Keys had mangrove swamps and coral reefs where a host of animals depended on ocean currents.

Both Paul Brooks and Carson's agent, Marie Rodell, were relieved that Carson had finally figured out how she wanted to write the book, even though it meant she had to rewrite much of the manuscript. In turn, this delayed the publication date, but by now editor and agent knew that Carson could not be rushed. Now that she finally had a structure she liked, Carson immersed herself in writing her third book, *The Edge of the Sea*.

Houghton Mifflin, the publisher, hired Carson's friend and former government colleague, Bob Hines, to draw illustrations for this seashore book. Bob and Carson spent many, many days together collecting specimens in tide pools and along beaches. Carson examined these creatures under a microscope and made notes about their structure and shape. Bob examined them too and

(left) **Carson and Bob Hines examining a sponge sample.**
Rex Gary Schmidt/By permission of Rachel Carson Council, Inc.

(below) **Paul Brooks, Carson's editor at Houghton Mifflin.**
Kate Brooks/Courtesy of the Walden Woods Project

drew exquisitely detailed and accurate pencil illustrations. When they were both finished, they took the creatures back to the shore to return them to their habitat.

Carson was so dedicated to her search for animals and plants to examine that she sometimes neglected herself. She frequently spent hours and hours standing in the water and got so cold that Bob would have to carry her back to her car where Maria had blankets ready.

At other times, Carson did the rescuing. Once, she spotted a dog mesmerized by something in the pools of water, way out on a sand bar at low tide. As the tide came in, the dog appeared not to notice. Concerned that the little fellow would become stranded, Carson waded out to him. The dog was chasing ghost shrimps in the pools and

couldn't be dissuaded from his task. So, Carson carried the dog closer to shore.

Another time, Carson and Marjorie went outside at midnight to watch waves crashing on the beach. A magnificent display of bioluminescence—a glowing light made by marine plankton—sparkled in the surf. Suddenly Carson noticed a firefly getting dangerously close to the water, presumably mistaking the glowing waves as others of its own kind. The firefly got trapped by the water's surface and blinked its light desperately. Carson

Carson examining a sea star.
By permission of Rachel Carson Council, Inc.

splashed toward it and scooped up the little fly, setting it in a child's sand pail to dry out.

Dear Dorothy

At the end of 1952, with her cottage on Southport Island well under construction, Carson received a letter from a Mrs. Dorothy Freeman, her soon-to-be neighbor. Dorothy and her husband, Stanley, had read *The Sea Around Us* and were thrilled that Carson owned a nearby property on Southport Island. Freeman had written to welcome Carson to the area, and Carson replied to say how much she looked forward to having a summer retreat where she could write in peace. She also invited Dorothy and Stanley to drop by the following summer when she and her mother moved in. Thus started a close friendship that continued till Carson's dying day.

When Rachel and Dorothy met in July 1953, they felt an immediate bond. They both revered nature and the ocean, and they also shared a love of cats. Later that summer, Carson took the Freemans to see the pools left behind by the low tide. They collected creatures to view under the microscope and, as always, later returned them to their watery homes. Before leaving to return to Maryland in the fall, Rachel wrote a note of farewell to Dorothy, and Dorothy did the same for Rachel. Over the winter, they wrote to each other almost daily. They became so emotionally close that they began writing two letters at a time. One was a "typical" letter that could be read aloud to Stanley (in Dorothy's case) or Maria (in Rachel's case), and

RACHEL L. CARSON'S *THE SEA AROUND US*

The documentary film of *The Sea Around Us* fell well short of Carson's hopes and expectations. She and Marie Rodell realized too late that the wording in the contract with the film producer left Carson out of the film's preparation. Although she could review the script, she couldn't make any changes to it. When she received the script, Carson read the bad grammar and scientific errors with disgust. She sent back pages of comments, and although the producer made some changes, the final version of the film had little resemblance to the book of its title.

When the film came out in 1953, it got mixed reviews. In a letter to her friend Dorothy Freeman, Carson said the *Washington Post*'s movie critic "roasted the script, for which I was duly grateful." Nevertheless, the film won an Oscar for best feature documentary at the 25th Academy Awards.

---

the other was a private letter just for Dorothy's or Rachel's eyes. They called the private letter an "apple," after a common toy at the time: a small wooden apple inside a larger one.

The Sea's Biographer

By 1954, when Carson had completed much of her manuscript for *The Edge of the Sea*, she received thrilling news from William Shawn, the editor of the *New Yorker*. He wanted to publish a short version of the book, just as he had done for *The Sea Around Us*. Shawn even told Rodell that Carson had "done it again," meaning that Carson had written another superb book.

Indeed, within only a few weeks of being published in October 1955, the new book had already leaped onto bestseller lists. As before, Carson and her book received rave reviews. She was clearly not a "one-hit wonder," but rather a writer who could produce magic each time her pen met paper (with many, many revisions, of course).

Ever since *The Sea Around Us* came out, Carson had been receiving honors. They continued for years after *The Edge of the Sea* appeared too. She was made an honorary fellow of the Boston Science Museum and received the Achievement Award of the American Association of University Women. Over these years, Carson also continued to give speeches. She spoke at the annual meeting of the American Association for the Advancement of Science (known as AAAS) and to members of the Audubon Society. Stanley Freeman, Dorothy's husband, loved taking nature photographs,

Dorothy Freeman. *Rachel Carson Papers, American Literature Collection, Beinecke Rare Book and Manuscript Library, Yale University*

Picture Earth's Water

We have a single planet Earth with everything needed to sustain life. Much of the planet is covered in water, yet only a small fraction of it is freshwater. An even smaller fraction is available to plants and animals (including humans).
In this activity, you will be able to picture how much (and how little) water exists on Earth.

ADULT SUPERVISION REQUIRED

You'll Need

➤ Apple

➤ Cutting board

➤ Knife

➤ Paper or thin cardboard (for labels)

➤ Pen or marker

➤ Pencil and paper (for notes)

➤ Measuring cup

➤ 1 liter of water

➤ Large glass bowl or measuring jug (that holds more than 1 liter of liquid)

➤ Food coloring

➤ Spoon

➤ Plastic syringe with markings for 5 mL or 10 mL

➤ 5 small bowls, glass if possible

Part 1

1. The apple represents the Earth. On the cutting board, cut it in quarters. Put one quarter aside with a label marked "land." This much of the Earth is covered by land.

2. Take another of the quarters and slice it in half (= ⅛) and in half again (= 1/16) and in half again (= 1/32) and—if you're able to—in half one last time (= 1/64).

3. Put one of the 1/64 sections aside with a label marked "freshwater." This much of the Earth is covered by freshwater.

4. Put the remaining two intact apple quarters and the rest of the sliced-up quarter in a pile together. Label them "oceans." This much of the Earth is covered by salt water.

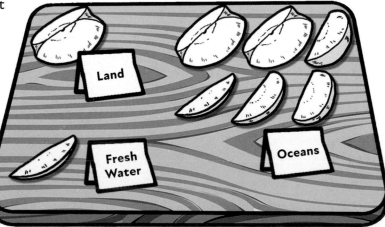

Part 2

5. Look closely at the skinny section of apple representing freshwater. Where do you think that freshwater is on Earth? Make a list of all the places you might find freshwater.

6. Use a measuring cup to pour 1 liter (1,000 mL) of water into a glass bowl or measuring jug. Drip a few drops of food coloring—any color—into the water and stir it around. This represents all the water on Earth, both salt and fresh.

7. Use a syringe to remove 25 mL from the bowl of water. Squirt it carefully into one of the small bowls. The large bowl now represents all the salt water on Earth, and the small bowl represents all the freshwater on Earth. Label the salt water.

8. From the small bowl, remove 17 mL of water and squirt it into another small bowl. Label it "icecaps and glaciers."

9. From the first small bowl, remove 7 mL of water and squirt it carefully into a third small bowl. Label it "underground freshwater" or "groundwater."

10. Take a look at what's left in the first small bowl—just 1 mL. Try to syringe up this remaining water and separate it into two more small bowls, one with ⅔ of the water and the other with ⅓ of the water. Label the bowl with ⅔ mL (0.66 mL) of water as "other" (includes soil moisture, water in the atmosphere, permafrost), and label the bowl with ⅓ mL (0.33 mL) of water as "rivers, lakes, and wetlands."

11. Now that you can picture where Earth's water is, write down your thoughts about people's relationship with water. Where do we get the water we use? How do we use water, and where does it go when we have finished using it? Which water sources do animals and plants use? How do we value water?

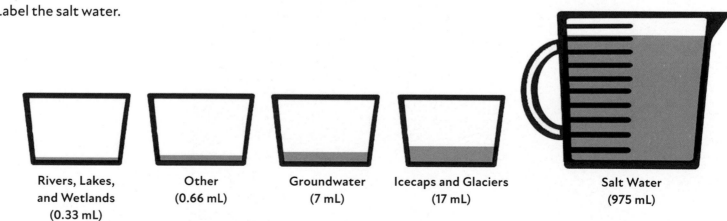

Rivers, Lakes, and Wetlands (0.33 mL)

Other (0.66 mL)

Groundwater (7 mL)

Icecaps and Glaciers (17 mL)

Salt Water (975 mL)

so he supplied Carson with slides to embellish her talks.

Dorothy and Stanley had become such an important part of Carson's life that she dedicated her book to these new friends: "To Dorothy and Stanley Freeman who have gone down with me into the low-tide world and have felt its beauty and its mystery."

Cycles in Nature

Because of her ability to write about science in an appealing way, Carson continued to be inundated with requests. Could she write about such and such? Would she speak to so-and-so's association?

The cottage Carson had built on Southport Island, Maine. *Freeman Family Collection, Edmund S. Muskie Archives and Special Collections Library, Bates College*

A few of them intrigued her. One was a request to write a television script about clouds, a topic suggested by an eight-year-old girl. Although Carson didn't own a television, she saw this as an opportunity to reach a large audience and to write about the big picture of life on Earth. After all, clouds don't exist "just because." They are part of the **water cycle**, which affects every living being on the planet.

A **cycle** means that something—water, in the case of the water cycle—is circulating from place to place and changing from one form to another. The water cycle involves water evaporating (changing from a liquid to a gas) into the atmosphere where it eventually cools, forms clouds, and then becomes rain or snow. This precipitation falls onto the land where it either soaks into the groundwater or runs off into a lake, stream, or ocean, ready to evaporate again and repeat the cycle. Plants contribute to the water cycle by taking water into their roots, moving it into their leaves, and then losing it to the air in a process called **transpiration** (evaporation from plant parts). Animals are also part of the water cycle by drinking water and then peeing and sweating it out. Humans play a large role in the water cycle since we take water for our own uses and then return it to the environment, often not as clean as when we took it.

There are many other cycles in nature—the carbon and nitrogen cycles, for example. Cycles in nature go around and around: nutrients get used, changed, recycled.

As with nearly everything Carson wrote, the clouds program sounded like poetry. A segment about the water cycle said, "yet in a constantly renewing cycle there is no end, as there is no beginning. Stage succeeds stage, turning again and again upon itself like a wheel." Carson even managed to compare the air to the ocean and people to deep-sea fishes: "We are going to pretend we live on the bottom of an ocean—an ocean of air in which clouds are adrift," she wrote. "We are exactly like deep-sea fishes, with all the weight of tons of air pressing down upon our bodies."

When the clouds program was broadcast on the show *Omnibus* with the title "Something About the Sky," Carson and her family watched it at her brother's house. Within a few days, Carson had bought her own television set, much to the delight of her mother, Maria.

Exploring with Roger

Another request that appealed to Carson was from a magazine called *Woman's Home Companion*. The editor asked if she would write an article to encourage adults to share outdoor experiences with children and take an interest in nature together. Carson loved this idea!

Thanks to her mother's influence all those years before, growing up on Colfax Hill in Springdale, Carson herself held a childlike wonder at the beauty and variety of the natural world. And ever since Roger—her niece Marjorie's son—had entered her life, Carson had delighted in sharing the world of plants and animals with him. Right from when he was a baby, Carson had taken Roger to the seashore to experience the sights, sounds,

and smells of the sea. She had also taken him into the woods behind her cottage to explore the forest floor and spot squirrels, woodpeckers, and other creatures.

For the article, Carson wrote about their adventures, describing how they used their senses—sight, smell, sound, and touch. Carson wrote about the little things that small children notice and grown-ups often ignore. "If I had influence with the good fairy who is supposed to preside over the christening of all children," she wrote, "I should ask that her gift to each child in the world be a sense of wonder so indestructible that it would last through life."

The article, "Help Your Child to Wonder," published in July 1956, brought both Maria and Marjorie to tears. Marie Rodell suggested that she turn the article into a book. Carson liked this idea but got sidetracked with other projects.

Thrust into Motherhood

In the fall of 1956, Maria Carson's health steadily worsened. She was by this time 88 years old. After Maria fell one October morning, Carson realized that she couldn't leave her mother alone. Once she had closed up their summer cottage and driven back to Maryland, Carson hired a housekeeper to cook and clean. Fortunately, Maria seemed to be content with this arrangement, provided she could direct the housekeeper's work.

A new year often brings hope and optimism, but the new year of 1957 brought more sadness for Carson and her small family. On January 15,

Carson with a child. *Rachel Carson Papers, American Literature Collection, Beinecke Rare Book and Manuscript Library, Yale University*

Make a Worm Farm

For many cycles in nature, one group of organisms—called the decomposers—plays a critical role. They feed on dead plants and animals. Their feeding activity decomposes, or breaks down, the dead material. As decomposers work, nutrients like nitrogen and phosphorus get changed back into forms that living plants can use. The decomposers are bacteria, fungi, and invertebrates like worms, snails, millipedes, and flies.

If you collect food scraps at home and put them in a compost bin, you know that over time, the scraps get broken down and eventually become dark, chunky soil that can be spread on a garden. Inside the compost bin, decomposers are hard at work eating, pooping, and changing nutrients from one form to another.

In this activity, you'll create a small indoor compost bin that will produce great fertilizer for plants.

You'll Need

- Clean plastic container with lid (750-mL yogurt container or larger)
- Thumbtack
- 2 sheets of newspaper
- ¼ cup of water
- Bowl or bucket that can get dirty
- 2 tablespoons of soil
- Handful of uncooked food scraps (vegetable peelings, apple cores, etc.)
- 4–5 red wiggler worms (available at bait stores, worm suppliers, or in a neighbor's compost bin)
- Wire rack, small rocks, or similar items for container to sit raised up
- Plate or tray to catch liquid

1. Use the thumbtack to make about 20 holes in the lid of the plastic container and another 20 holes in its bottom.

2. Tear the newspaper into strips, put them in the bowl, and moisten them with water. They should be the dampness of a wrung-out sponge. Add the soil and mix around. Un-clump the newspaper strips if needed.

3. Fill about 3/4 of the plastic container with dirty, un-clumped, moist newspaper. Don't pack it in tightly; the worms need air.

4. Place a few bits of food waste on top of the newspaper and cover with another few strips of dirty, moist paper.

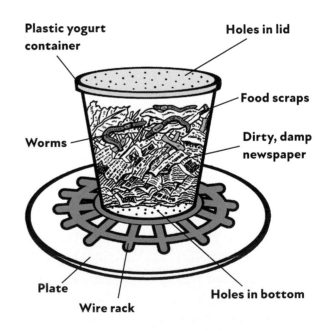

Plastic yogurt container — Holes in lid — Food scraps — Dirty, damp newspaper — Holes in bottom — Wire rack — Plate — Worms

5. Gently place the worms on top of the newspaper. They will start tunneling right away to get away from the light. Put the lid on the container.

6. Place a rack or several rocks on a plate or tray and perch the container on top to allow liquid to seep out the bottom.

7. Keep the worm farm in a warm location. Outdoors is fine in mild climates; indoors is best in cool and very hot climates. Check the farm every few days and give the worms more food scraps. **Only give fruit and vegetable scraps, no meat, grease, or fat.** If the container seems to be getting too dry, spray a little water or add some moist food like melon rinds.

8. Be patient! The work of decomposers can take time.

9. As your worms work, they will produce castings that look like soil. The castings are great fertilizer for plants. Liquid will also drip from the bottom of the container. Mix 1 part worm farm liquid with 10 parts water and use the mixture as a liquid fertilizer to water plants.

Optional: Use the same method but scaled up to build a larger worm farm in a tote bin to compost the fruit and vegetable waste from a classroom or entire household.

her niece Marjorie was admitted to hospital with pneumonia. A week later she came home and seemed to be getting better, but on January 30, she suddenly took a downward turn. She was rushed back to the hospital. Even so, within hours, she was dead. Marjorie, just 31 years old, left behind her son, Roger, only a few weeks from his fifth birthday.

Carson, who loved her niece like a little sister, was devastated. Not only did she have her own grief to deal with, she had her elderly mother to attend to and now a young child to care for as well. It might have made sense for Marjorie's older sister, Virginia, to take Roger, but Virginia and her husband didn't care for the idea of raising a youngster. After his mother, Carson and Maria were the two people Roger knew best. There was nothing else for it: Carson and her mother decided they would raise the little boy.

Given Maria's age and health, it was really Carson who took on this responsibility. She adopted Roger, making her grandnephew her son as well. Carson, at nearly age 50, had embarked on motherhood. She despaired about her lack of parenting experience as well as the limited time she could now devote to her research and writing. She described her anxieties and discouragement in letters to Dorothy. Meanwhile, she got on with life and raising Roger as best she could.

7

EVERYTHING IS CONNECTED

"Wildlife . . . is dwindling because its home is being destroyed. But the home of wildlife is also our home."
—Rachel Carson, "Fight for Wildlife Pushes Ahead," *Richmond Times-Dispatch Sunday Magazine*, 1938

In the 1940s and '50s, science and technology were bringing exciting inventions to ordinary people. Jet airplanes made travel faster; an undersea telephone cable made calls between North America and Europe easier. The booming economy after World War II meant that Americans could afford to buy things like televisions and automatic washing machines. Numerous products made life more convenient: disposable diapers,

A crop duster plane releasing pesticides over fields. *Gado Images/Alamy Stock Photo*

kitty litter, and bug sprays. The public lapped up these new wonder-products, which manufacturers told them were safe to use.

The Nuclear Age

From a scientific standpoint, the remarkable achievements of the 1940s and '50s impressed many people. However, some of the new technologies disturbed Rachel Carson. She had once thought humans could never change certain parts of Earth—the sky, the ocean. Now she realized how naive she had been, especially when news broke of another huge stride: scientists had learned how to split an atom in a process called nuclear fission. By splitting atoms, they could create a new class of destructive bombs. The nuclear age had begun.

The world's first nuclear explosion happened on July 16, 1945, in the New Mexico desert. This explosion was a test. The next month, in August 1945, near the end of World War II, the United States exploded two atom bombs over Japan—one over the city of Hiroshima and the other over Nagasaki. Both explosions caused terrible loss of life and hideous radiation illnesses in the victims who survived the blasts. Other countries started building nuclear weapons too, and for the next two decades they triggered hundreds of test explosions around the world.

When an atom bomb explodes above ground, it shoots dangerous, radioactive particles into the atmosphere. Larger particles—looking like ash or snow—fall back to Earth. Lighter particles move around in the atmosphere and gradually

The mushroom cloud resulting from a nuclear test explosion at Bikini Atoll in the Marshall Islands, Pacific Ocean, in 1946. *Pictorial Press Ltd/Alamy Stock Photo*

return to Earth in rainfall and other precipitation. This nuclear fallout releases dangerous energy that harms or even kills animals and plants. Strontium 90, the name of one type of radioactive particle, became part of the public's everyday vocabulary. Scientists discovered it in large amounts in cow's milk and baby teeth. People all over the world began to fear nuclear fallout and the damaging effects on themselves, their children, and their communities.

Controlling Diseases and Pests

Nuclear fallout wasn't the only danger in the air in the 1940s and '50s. After World War II, trucks began roaming streets, parks, and beaches spraying chemical **pesticides** to kill disease-carrying insects such as mosquitoes that transmitted malaria. Spraying programs also targeted house flies that people thought (incorrectly) carried the polio virus. The "fog trucks," as people called them, sprayed several substances, including DDT, the chemical Carson had wanted to write about for *Reader's Digest* magazine in 1945. Officials claimed that DDT was a gift from World War II research and wasn't harmful to humans. Carson had her doubts.

Later, Carson became alarmed by a program conducted by the US Department of Agriculture to spray farmers' fields. In this case, the target was fire ants, which had been unintentionally introduced into the United States from South America in the 1930s and had spread through many southern states. As their name implies, fire ants have

MOVE OVER, TOOTH FAIRY!

The Baby Tooth Survey began in 1959. Dr. Louise Reiss led the project to collect teeth and measure how much strontium 90 they contained. Scientists suspected this radioactive material from nuclear bomb testing was getting into the food supply.

Strontium 90 has a chemical structure similar to calcium, so the body stores strontium 90 in bones and teeth. Once there, it lets out radiation that can damage soft tissues and increase a person's chance of developing cancer later in life.

The Baby Tooth Survey ran for 12 years and collected about 300,000 teeth from children in the St. Louis, Missouri, area. In exchange for their teeth, children received a button and membership in "Operation Tooth Club." Other surveys began elsewhere in the United States and Canada.

Because the world's first-ever nuclear bomb explosion happened in July 1945, the project wanted teeth from before and after this date. The results showed about 100 times more strontium 90 in baby teeth from after 1945 compared with baby teeth from before 1945.

As the results came in, they were reported to the government. The baby tooth project contributed to President John F. Kennedy's decision to negotiate a Nuclear Test Ban Treaty with the Soviet Union and Britain. The ban began in 1963, and for children born just five years later, the amount of strontium 90 in their teeth was already lower.

Children who donated their teeth for science received a button. *Smithsonian National Museum of American History*

A truck spraying DDT at a public beach in New York in 1945. Note the wording on the side of the truck.
Pictorial Press Ltd/Alamy Stock Photo

that the spraying was poisoning their land, while killing birds, insects, and fish. Carson knew some of the Long Island residents, and she followed the progress of this legal battle with great interest.

Birth of a New Project

At this time—late 1957—Carson toyed with writing ideas. Without a new book project, she was pondering what she might work on. She wrote a magazine article about the seashore and many, many letters to Dorothy Freeman. It then occurred to her that perhaps she should revisit her idea to write a magazine article about pesticides and their effects on wildlife.

a painful sting. Farmers complained that these insects were devastating both their livestock and crops. The Department of Agriculture responded by spraying pesticides, sometimes DDT and sometimes even more potent chemicals, from airplanes flying low over fields. Carson feared for the wildlife living on or near these fields. What would DDT and other chemical pesticides do to them?

Carson also read about a lawsuit involving pesticides. Several residents of Long Island, New York, sued the Department of Agriculture because their properties had been sprayed with chemicals without their permission. The goal on Long Island was to get rid of Dutch elm disease, caused by a fungus and spread by a beetle. The Long Islanders who filed the lawsuit were organic gardeners who never used chemicals on their crops. They claimed

As Carson considered this idea, aerial spraying programs against tent caterpillars, gypsy moths, and mosquitoes infuriated more and more people. Some of them wrote angry letters to local newspapers. Olga Owens Huckins went a step further. She sent an angry letter to a newspaper and a copy of her letter to Carson. Huckins, herself a writer, and Carson had corresponded in the past about Carson's sea books. After Carson and her mother, Maria, read Olga's letter and some of the other angry letters published in newspapers, Maria became furious at the needless deaths of songbirds. She telephoned the White House to complain!

For Carson, these stories about the disastrous effects of pesticide spraying on wildlife focused her mind. She began making telephone calls of her own, not to the White House, but to various government departments, asking for information. She also wrote to Marjorie Spock, one of the two women who had launched the Long Island lawsuit. Spock was thrilled that the much-admired writer Rachel Carson was interested in their case. She sent Carson the first of several packages of information. Over the months to follow, she also got Carson in touch with numerous scientists and doctors.

Carson was by now quite certain that she should write an article on the dangers of pesticides, but no magazine seemed interested in the topic. Marie Rodell, Carson's agent, contacted numerous magazine editors and received the same negative response every time. Carson and Rodell discussed what to do and thought that writing a short book might be the answer. Rodell asked Paul Brooks, Carson's editor for *The Edge of the Sea*, and finally the answer was positive. Yes, Brooks was interested in a book about the dangers of pesticides. He even suggested a title: *The Control of Nature*.

With the project taking shape in her mind, Carson kept collecting information. She also wisely hired a research assistant to help gather, read, and summarize the growing pile of research studies and articles. Carson's first idea—to write about pesticides harming wildlife—grew over time to include the dangers for people as well. The pesticide DDT was by this time in widespread use in home products across the United States to kill "nuisance" bugs—mosquitoes, biting flies, roaches, and the like.

In the piles of paper growing on Carson's desk were studies looking into health risks for people exposed to chemicals in their environment. As she researched and read, Carson added a host of other

The great expectations held for DDT have been realized. During 1946, exhaustive scientific tests have shown that, when properly used, DDT kills a host of destructive insect pests, and is a benefactor of all humanity.

Pennsalt produces DDT and its products in all standard forms and is now one of the country's largest producers of this amazing insecticide. Today, everyone can enjoy added comfort, health and safety through the insect-killing powers of Pennsalt DDT products . . . and DDT is only one of Pennsalt's many chemical products which benefit industry, farm and home.

GOOD FOR STEERS—Beef grows meatier nowadays . . . for it's a scientific fact that—compared to untreated cattle—beef-steers gain up to 50 pounds extra when protected from horn flies and many other pests with DDT insecticides.

GOOD FOR FRUITS—Bigger apples, juicier fruits that are free from unsightly worms . . . all benefits resulting from DDT dusts and sprays.

Knox Out FOR THE HOME—helps to make healthier, more comfortable homes . . . protects your family from dangerous insect pests. Use Knox-Out DDT Powders and Sprays as directed . . . then watch the bugs "bite the dust"!

Knox Out FOR DAIRIES—Up to 20% more milk . . . more butter . . . more cheese . . . tests prove greater milk production when dairy cows are protected from the annoyance of many insects with DDT insecticides like Knox-Out Stock and Barn Spray.

GOOD FOR ROW CROPS—25 more barrels of potatoes per acre . . . actual DDT tests have shown crop increases like this! DDT dusts and sprays help truck farmers pass these gains along to you.

Knox Out FOR INDUSTRY—Food processing plants, laundries, dry cleaning plants, hotels . . . dozens of industries gain effective bug control, more pleasant work conditions with Pennsalt DDT products.

PENN SALT CHEMICALS
97 Years' Service to Industry • Farm • Home

PENNSYLVANIA SALT MANUFACTURING COMPANY
WIDENER BUILDING, PHILADELPHIA 7, PA.

A magazine ad promoting the beneficial uses of DDT. *Courtesy of Science History Institute*

chemical pesticides to her list, chemicals with names like chlordane, heptachlor, endrin, and dieldrin. Carson also began thinking about the parallels between nuclear fallout and widespread pesticide spraying. Both, she realized, were often invisible, yet they could travel great distances in the environment and have severe consequences for wildlife and people exposed to them. The title of Carson's book manuscript changed to *Man Against Nature*.

Nature's Connections

As with all her previous writing, Carson wanted to emphasize the connections among all living things, humans included. She felt people needed to understand how misuse of pesticides could harm the relationships between different players in an ecosystem.

All ecological relationships are dynamic—they change over time. Ecosystems left to nature's whims experience constant give and take and constant gain and loss, yet they generally have time to adapt to changing circumstances. For example, perhaps an ideal combination of warm air and moist soil encourages a particular kind of plant to thrive. The abundant plants provide lots of food for some herbivore, and many of the herbivore's babies survive because they're well fed. As the herbivore population grows bigger, though, the many herbivores eat more and more of the plants—a loss to this plant population. But this makes way for a different kind of plant to grow, and perhaps the new plant is a favorite of an insect species, which

then gains as well. This is just a simple example of how relationships between players in an ecosystem are dynamic, or ever-changing.

This balancing act can be disrupted if a dramatic event happens. After an event like an earthquake or forest fire, the ecosystem is set to a new beginning. Nature then starts re-creating that ecosystem. Plant seeds blow in and germinate, roots that survived send up suckers, insects fly in, animals wander in. Slowly a new ecosystem develops and goes through stages in a process called **ecological succession** to become a mature ecosystem again. Nature works to regain balance.

Applying pesticides over broad areas of land and water is an example of a human action that disrupts nature's balance. These chemicals harm or kill many species and many individuals all at once. For her new book project, Carson wrote about examples of birds and animals turning up dead after spray planes had passed overhead. In one chapter, she described a community in Illinois sprayed with dieldrin to snuff out an invasive beetle. Scores of animals died, including earthworms, robins, meadowlarks, pheasants, rabbits, and ground squirrels. Domestic animals like cats and sheep also became sick or died. In another example, DDT spraying in eastern Canada to control the spruce budworm covered thousands of acres of trees. Within only a few days of the spraying, birds died in the forests, as did insects and salmon in the streams. Because these chemicals were affecting many more species than the targeted pests, Carson believed that the chemicals shouldn't be called "pesticides," "insecticides," or "**herbicides**," but rather **biocides**. In these words, *–cide* comes from a Latin word meaning "cut" or "kill."

An Accumulating Problem

Carson also described how the relationships between animals in an ecosystem can be an animal's undoing. Say earthworms absorb a chemical from the soil, and then a robin eats one of these worms and some of the chemical gets into the robin's body. The robin eats another chemical worm, and another, and another. Its body starts to accumulate, or build up, more and more of the chemical. This is called **bioaccumulation**. Say now that a fox **preys** on this robin and on five other birds that also ate chemical earthworms. The fox accumulates an even larger amount of the chemical. This building up of the chemical from one level in the food chain to the next is called **biomagnification**. Apex species at the top of food pyramids suffer from the most intense buildup of dangerous chemicals.

As well as killing animals, chemical pesticides can have subtler (but no less damaging) effects. For example, scientists realized that the bald eagle—an **apex predator**—was in trouble. In the late 1700s, bald eagles numbered in the tens of thousands. By the 1940s and '50s, this majestic bird—the national emblem of the United States—was in danger of extinction.

There were several reasons for their decline. Loss of nesting habitat and illegal shooting were two of them. A third had to do with ecosystem connections and biomagnification. Bald eagles primarily eat fish, and when they began eating fish contaminated with DDT, the chemical built up in the eagles' bodies. The DDT made their eggshells very thin. With weak shells, the eggs broke as the heavy adult birds sat on the eggs to incubate them. Sometimes the shells didn't break but the chicks never hatched from the eggs, or they hatched and soon died. Instead of affecting the birds exposed to it, the DDT harmed the next generation.

Later, several years after Carson's death, the bald eagles' fortune improved. With national laws to protect these birds and their nests, plus captive breeding programs and a ban on DDT, their numbers began climbing. By 2007 more than 9,000 pairs nested in the United States, not including Alaska and Hawaii. The bald eagle recovery is a truly remarkable story, repeated for ospreys, peregrine falcons, hawks, brown pelicans, and other birds whose eggshells are affected by DDT.

Chemical Staying Power

DDT and many of the other pesticides Carson wrote about in her pesticide book are in a class known as **persistent organic pollutants**, or POPs. *Persistent* means they take a long time to break down in the environment (sometimes decades), *organic* means they have carbon and hydrogen atoms bonded to each other as part of their basic structure, and *pollutants* means they are toxic to humans and wildlife. Carson was referring to this problem of persistence when she wrote in her pesticide book, "No one yet knows what the ultimate consequences may be."

A bald eagle with a meal. *iStock.com BrianEKushner*

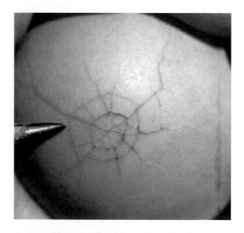

A pencil tip pointing at cracks in an egg with a thin shell due to DDT. *USGS Patuxent Wildlife Research Center*

Build a Balanced Ecosystem

An ecosystem is a community of biotic and abiotic things that live in a particular area. The losses and gains—or the give and take—of all the different parts of an ecosystem keep it functioning. What one thing loses or gives, another thing gains or takes. For example, an animal takes in oxygen and gives out carbon dioxide. A plant does the opposite. You can create a mini, enclosed ecosystem at home to observe how this works.

You'll Need

- 1 liter of water (dechlorinated if tap water—see Step 1)
- Shallow pan to dechlorinate tap water
- 2 2-liter clear plastic bottles
- Marker
- Scissors
- Aquarium gravel or small pebbles
- A few fronds of a pond plant (such as *Elodea*, duckweed, or another variety available at a pet/aquarium store)
- 2–4 small freshwater animals such as guppy fish or snails (available at a pet/aquarium store)
- Strong elastic band and netting (old pantyhose works well)
- Garden soil or potting soil
- 6–8 seeds (rye and alfalfa work well)
- 2–3 leaves and 2 small sticks
- 1–2 land animals such as pill bugs or an earthworm
- Clear packing tape
- Paper or notebook and pencil
- Camera (optional)

1. If using tap water, dechlorinate it by letting it sit in a shallow pan, open to the air, for 24 hours.

2. Use the marker to draw cutting lines around the bottles. Cut carefully with scissors to end up with three sections, as shown to the right.

3. In the bottom piece, place an inch of gravel. Fill with dechlorinated water to about three inches from the top cut edge of the bottle. Add the pond plants and the pond animals.

4. Remove the bottle cap from the large top piece and turn it upside down. Cover the opening with netting and attach it securely with an elastic band.

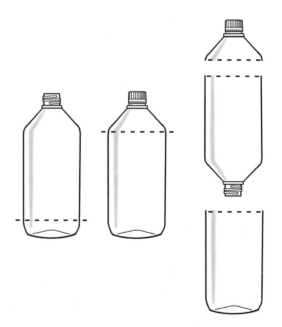

5. Add an inch of gravel, three inches of soil, seeds, leaves, sticks, and the land animal(s).

6. Slip the small top piece half an inch down inside the cut edge and attach it with packing tape. Leave its cap attached.

7. Slip the upside-down bottle into the bottom piece and attach them with packing tape.

8. Place the mini-ecosystem in a bright spot where the plants can get light for photosynthesis. Avoid a spot that's very hot or very cold. You might need to move your ecosystem around till you find a location that seems to suit it well.

9. Make notes about your mini-ecosystem when you first set it up and take a photo if you have a camera available to you. Then, once a week, make more notes and take another photo to track how each part of the ecosystem is doing.

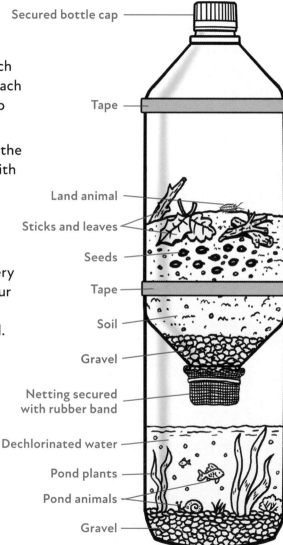

Secured bottle cap
Tape
Land animal
Sticks and leaves
Seeds
Tape
Soil
Gravel
Netting secured with rubber band
Dechlorinated water
Pond plants
Pond animals
Gravel

In discussing chemical persistence and long-term effects on humans, Carson drew on work by Dr. Wilhelm Hueper, one of the first scientists in the United States to study cancers resulting from people's occupations and the environment. When Carson corresponded with him to gather information for her book, he was working at the National Cancer Institute. Earlier in his career, he had worked for DuPont, a chemical manufacturer. There, he had gathered data suggesting that DuPont workers were getting bladder cancer from working with certain industrial dyes. The company tried to censor, or cover up, Hueper's warning and eventually fired him. He continued his work elsewhere on cancer-causing agents, known as **carcinogens**. One of the chemicals he called a carcinogen was DDT.

Carson also reported the work of doctors from the respected Mayo Clinic where more and more patients were coming in with blood disorders, including leukemia, which is cancer of the bone marrow and other blood-forming tissues. One Mayo Clinic doctor discovered that most of these patients had been exposed to pesticide sprays. Some developed acute leukemia and died within days. In telling these stories, Carson compared the effects of pesticide exposure with the effects of nuclear fallout. Both can cause sudden and extreme illness.

The People Around Her

Throughout her search for facts and the numbers to back them up, Carson remained convinced

POPS GO PLACES

Persistent organic pollutants, or POPs, are chemicals that raise concerns all over the world. They include DDT and aldrin (used as pesticides) and others such as polychlorinated biphenyls (PCBs) and dioxins (used in industrial processes). Four characteristics of these chemicals make them dangerous:

1. They accumulate in plants and animals and biomagnify up food chains. This means that apex predators—animals at the top of food chains—have especially high amounts of POPs in their bodies. For example, PCBs contaminate the blubber of many orcas (also known as killer whales) throughout the world's oceans.

2. They persist—stick around without breaking down—for a long time. DDT can take as long as 20 years to break down into a different form. Even then, the broken-down form, called by the letters DDE, is still harmful to animals.

3. They get into water, soil, and the air and travel all over the planet, often far from where they first entered the environment. Thanks to being transported on air currents high above the Earth's surface, many POPs have made their way to the planet's poles. Scientists have measured large amounts of POPs in the breast milk of mothers living in the High Arctic.

4. They affect the health of animals, including humans, by increasing cancer risk, causing reproduction problems, changing the immune system, affecting the brain, and more. For example, a study in 2012 looked at the risk of breast cancer for women whose mother had been exposed to DDT while pregnant. The adult daughters of the moms exposed to a lot of DDT were at higher risk of developing breast cancer.

that the public needed to know the dangers of pesticides. Her mother, Maria, agreed and wholeheartedly supported her daughter's new book project. But Carson's friend Dorothy Freeman felt conflicted. Dorothy loved Carson's poetic writing about the sea. Pesticides, on the other hand, seemed like a terribly negative subject. Dorothy also couldn't participate in a pesticide book in the same way she had with *The Edge of the Sea*. Exploring tide pools brought Dorothy such joy and a closeness to Carson, but there was little, if anything, that Dorothy could contribute to a book about poisons.

Dorothy's misgivings didn't deter Carson. She simply did her best to explain to her dear friend how important this new book project had become to her. In a letter, Carson wrote that she could never again be at peace unless she spoke out.

Paul Brooks understood Carson's passion, and he also understood the importance of a book's title. It had to connect with readers. Carson, Rodell, and Brooks weren't happy with the *Man Against Nature* title. They exchanged other title ideas, but nothing seemed right. Later, in fall 1960, Brooks read the chapter on birds and suggested "Silent Spring" as the chapter title. Carson said that seemed fine.

But they still couldn't come up with a good book title. Rodell also read the bird chapter, loved it, and loved its title even more. She suggested that the whole book be titled *Silent Spring*. Nothing was decided. A few months later, Brooks again proposed *Silent Spring*, this time echoing Rodell's idea that it title the entire book, not just the bird chapter. Carson still wasn't sure.

Goodbye, Maria

In November 1958, Maria Carson's health took another downward turn. She had a stroke followed by pneumonia. The end was near, and Carson knew it.

On Maria's final night, Carson sat by her bedside, occasionally wandering to the window to look at the twinkling stars. In the early morning, with Carson holding her hand, Maria drew her last breath. The woman who had introduced Carson to the natural world, who had given up so much and pushed so hard for Carson to get an education, who had been Carson's near-constant companion and helper, was gone. Carson mourned.

In the new year, knowing how passionately her mother had believed in the pesticide book, Carson plunged back into her research and writing. Given the wide look she had decided to take, Carson was reading up on the latest information in many different subjects. She read about chemistry, cell biology, and cancer. Throughout all her research, she kept careful notes. She had done this with her ocean projects too, but Carson knew this book was in a class of its own. It would make waves and spark hostile responses. She was determined to have every single one of her facts accurate and documented.

Hard though it must have been to lose her mother, there was some consolation for Carson. She could more freely spend time with friends rather than constantly worrying about her mother's sensitive feelings. For one, Carson's relationship with Marie Rodell became easier after Maria's death.

Carson and Dorothy. *Freeman Family Collection/Courtesy of Linda Lear Center for Special Collections and Archives, Connecticut College*

Maria and Rodell had never gotten along particularly well. Carson also no longer had to attend to the daily care and attention her mother demanded.

On the other hand, Carson was now the sole caregiver for Roger, her grandnephew and adopted son. The summer of 1959 was their first at the Southport cottage without Maria. Initially Carson had high hopes for a productive few months, since Roger was at a day camp, leaving Carson with the entire day in which to work. After little more than a week of camp, though, Roger became seriously ill with a lung condition. Once again, Carson sacrificed her writing to play the familiar role of nurse.

Turkey Without Cranberry Sauce

Although frustrated by her slow progress, Carson knew she had to keep writing. A public health scare in the fall of 1959 emphasized that her concerns

See Bioaccumulation and Biomagnification in Action

In her writing, Rachel Carson gave several examples of bioaccumulation and biomagnification. In this activity, you will simulate how bioaccumulation and biomagnification happen.

You'll Need

- Empty egg carton
- Scissors
- Marker
- 100 candies: 75 of one color (color A) and 25 of a different color (color B). Skittles or jellybeans work well. All 100 candies must be of the same type (size, shape).
- Container to hold 100 candies
- Pencil
- A photocopy of the chart shown here
- Two dice
- Four small bowls
- One large bowl

Organism	Simulation	DDT in each individual	Total DDT	Divided by total number of individuals	Average DDT per individual	Average DDT per individual from three simulations
Phytoplankton	1		25	/100 =	1/4 or .25	
	2		25	/100 =	1/4 or .25	.25
	3		25	/100 =	1/4 or .25	
Zooplankton	1	_ + _ + _ + _ + _ + _ + _ + _ =		/9 =		
	2	_ + _ + _ + _ + _ + _ + _ + _ =		/9 =		
	3	_ + _ + _ + _ + _ + _ + _ + _ =		/9 =		
Fish	1	_ + _ + _ + _ =		/4 =		
	2	_ + _ + _ + _ =		/4 =		
	3	_ + _ + _ + _ =		/4 =		
Eagle	1	_ =		/1 =		
	2	_ =		/1 =		
	3	_ =		/1 =		

1. Cut out the egg carton so you have twelve individual cups. Discard three, and for the remaining nine cups, label each one on the outside using the numbers 2 through 10.

2. Put 100 candies into a container. The 75 color A candies represent uncontaminated phytoplankton. The 25 color B candies represent phytoplankton containing the pesticide known as DDT. The chart shows that 25/100 or 1/4 of the phytoplankton have DDT in them. Therefore, the amount of DDT in the phytoplankton population is 0.25 per individual.

3. Group the egg cups (order doesn't matter) on a table. The egg cups represent zooplankton, which eat phytoplankton. Close your eyes and randomly take 10 candies from the container and put them into one of the egg cups. Repeat until all nine egg cups have 10 candies each. (Ten candies will be left in the container.)

4. Count and record how many color B candies are in each egg cup. In other words, how many DDT-phytoplankton each zooplankton ate. Calculate the average amount of DDT in the zooplankton, as shown on the chart.

5. Roll the dice to randomly choose two egg cups to fill each of the four small bowls. The small bowls represent fish that eat zooplankton. If you roll a number that's already been used, keep rolling until you get the number of a cup not yet used. Ignore rolls of 11 and 12. (One egg cup will be left unused.)

6. Count and record how many color B candies are in each small bowl. In other words, how much DDT each fish has ingested from the zooplankton it ate. Calculate the average amount of DDT in the fish, as shown on the chart.

7. Group the four small bowls on the table, close your eyes, and move them about so you don't know which bowl is where. Keeping your eyes closed, pick up two of the bowls. Open your eyes and empty the two bowls into the large bowl, which represents an eagle. (Two small bowls will be left unused.)

8. Count and record how many color B candies are in the large bowl. In other words, how much DDT the eagle has ingested from the fish it ate. Record the number in the chart.

9. Return all the candies to the large container and repeat the simulation two more times. Calculate the average of the three trials for each organism in the food chain.

10. What do your results show? Which organism had the most DDT at the end of the experiment? Why did this happen?

about pesticides were real and important. As Thanksgiving approached, the country suddenly flew into a panic. Newspaper headlines screamed that cranberries—a staple of the traditional turkey dinner—were unsafe to eat!

The Great Cranberry Scare happened because a few West Coast farmers applied chemical herbicides to cranberry plants at the wrong time in the berries' growth. Some chemicals remained on the berries when farmers harvested them. The head of the government's health department declared these cranberries unfit to eat. Even though berries from other parts of the country weren't contaminated, the bags of cranberries and cans of sauce in grocery stores all looked the same. People didn't buy them, and many grocery stores took cranberry products off the shelves.

The incident devastated the cranberry industry that year, and it made the Department of Agriculture look incompetent for not having adequate regulations. For Carson, it provided a well-timed example of the possible dangers of pesticide use in farming. It also boosted the public's awareness of food safety.

Because of the Great Cranberry Scare and other newspaper headlines, including those about the plunging bald eagle population, Carson's confidence in her message grew. That fall she got on a roll with her writing. She had solid evidence to build her case and had several chapters written. As she finished chapters, she sent them to scientists for review and comment.

Through Rodell, chapters also went to William Shawn, editor at the *New Yorker* magazine.

In December Shawn called to tell Carson how excited he was about her writing and her message. Thrilled, Carson rang in the new decade—the 1960s—certain that a good year lay ahead, a year in which she would finish and publish the book that she now thought of as the most important work she had done. However, the year didn't unfold quite as she imagined.

A Race Against Time

In January, Carson suffered from an ulcer in her intestine. Then she got viral pneumonia, and then a sinus infection. For days at a time, she couldn't do any work. Next, she found two lumps in her left breast, so in March they were removed surgically. The doctor claimed that the lumps were **benign** (not cancerous), but even so, he removed Carson's whole breast—a procedure called a mastectomy. Since the doctor didn't recommend any further treatment, Carson was satisfied that the mastectomy had been an appropriate procedure and just a precaution. Thinking all was well, she focused on her recovery and returned to writing. It didn't last for long.

In the fall, Carson discovered another lump, this one between two of her ribs. Her doctor said he wasn't sure what this lump was or where it had come from, but he recommended **radiation treatment**. The treatment made her so ill that she decided to get a second opinion. She wrote to an acquaintance, Dr. George Crile, a cancer specialist. He requested Carson's medical records and discovered that Carson's surgeon had lied to her. The lumps removed the previous winter *had* been **malignant** (cancerous), and the doctors had known it at the time.

It seems incomprehensible now that even when Carson asked if the lumps were malignant, she was told they weren't. In the 1950s, it was common practice to discuss a woman's health with her husband, not with the woman herself. Since Carson didn't have a husband, perhaps the doctors decided it was best just not to discuss her condition at all. Crile, on the other hand, told Carson the truth: she had breast cancer, and the cancer had spread. He also recommended radiation treatment and found a different radiologist to administer it.

As well as interrupting her work, Carson's poor health brought time sharply into focus. She realized her time was limited, though how limited, she didn't know. But now more than ever, she knew she had to finish writing her pesticide book. Carson told Brooks and Rodell about her health problems but insisted that the news be kept private. She had no desire to see her private life discussed publicly, and she also worried that critics might relate her diagnosis to the points about carcinogens she planned to discuss in her book.

Sadly, Carson's health woes weren't over yet. In early 1961, while her radiation treatments were underway, she became ill with a bacterial infection that lodged in her knee and ankle joints. For weeks, she couldn't walk and was too ill and weak to write.

By springtime, Carson could muster the energy to return to her writing. The summer at her Maine cottage went well too, and the manuscript got closer to being complete. At the end of the summer, when Rodell visited Carson in Maine, she brought up the book's title again. Rodell was by now certain that *Silent Spring* fit the book beautifully. Carson still hesitated, until Rodell quoted some lines from a poem written by John Keats, an English poet. The lines went like this:

> *Though the sedge is withered from the lake,*
> *And no birds sing.*

On hearing that, Carson was persuaded. Her new book's title would be *Silent Spring*.

One last medical challenge awaited Carson before the year was out. In November, her irises—the colored parts of the eye—became swollen. This condition, called iritis, caused Carson severe pain, and even worse, she temporarily lost her sight.

Not being able to read her manuscript, she instead listened to it. Her assistant, Jeanne Davis, read it aloud and Carson dictated the changes she wanted to make.

Finally, in January 1962, when William Shawn at the *New Yorker* received the bulk of the manuscript to read, it struck a chord with him. He telephoned Carson and told her matter-of-factly that her work was "a brilliant achievement." Carson, who had always thought Shawn a superb editor, highly valued his opinion.

That evening, after Roger was asleep, Carson sat on the floor of her study with her cat Jeffie, and she cried. Four years of research, writing, and setback after setback were behind her. She had finished writing *Silent Spring*.

WHEN BIRDS CAN'T SING

> "No witchcraft, no enemy action had silenced the rebirth of new life in this stricken world. The people had done it themselves." —Rachel Carson, *Silent Spring*, 1962

As Rachel Carson was writing *Silent Spring*, she knew the material was complicated. It involved chemistry, biology, and statistics. But she wasn't writing the book for scientists. She wanted all sorts of people to read and understand the issues she was raising.

Carson excelled at beautiful writing in her earlier books about the ocean, and although *Silent Spring* had such a different core, she still managed to write elegantly. She used examples that struck readers' emotions, examples of real people affected by exposure to chemical pesticides. She also used literary devices like metaphors, where words are

Carson testifying in June 1963 before the government committee studying pesticides. *AP Photo* used to make comparisons. For example, she used chapter titles like "Earth's Green Mantle" and "Rivers of Death."

Carson also began the book with a chapter titled "A Fable for Tomorrow." In this fable, she described an imaginary town with flowering plants, abundant wildlife, and productive farms. Disaster struck this town after a "white powder" fell from the sky. Bees no longer buzzed through apple orchards, birds no longer sang, farm animals produced sickly young, and people became ill and some died. Near the end of the fable, Carson explained that no single town had experienced all these events, but each one had happened somewhere in the United States.

What Carson made plain in her fable is people's connection to nature. We live in human-built environments, but we rely on nature for survival. We can't live without clean water to drink, without plants that produce oxygen for us to breathe, without bees and birds that pollinate plants for us to eat, and on and on. The many things that nature provides, and we too often take for granted, are called **ecosystem services**. This term didn't exist in Carson's day, but the idea that every living thing contributes to and needs the web of life runs through *Silent Spring*.

A Noisy Reception

In mid-June 1962, the *New Yorker* magazine published the first of three installments of *Silent Spring*. Together, they were a short version of the full book that would come out later in the year.

As soon as the first installment ran, the *New Yorker*'s office was flooded with mail. Many readers were astonished by Carson's words. Some thanked her for bringing pesticide abuse to light, and others expressed fury at government departments and chemical companies. Other readers reacted with hostility. They criticized Carson's claims and some even took aim at her, declaring that only a woman could be so afraid of insects and that an unmarried, childless woman had no reason to care about future generations.

Carson knew *Silent Spring* would provoke controversy. By this point in her career, she had experience with receiving attention for her writing, although not with the fury some readers expressed. She felt confident that the information in her book was backed up by scientific studies, but all the same, she worried that pesticide companies would sue her or her publisher. Lawyers for the *New Yorker* and Houghton Mifflin reviewed the manuscript, and Carson herself double-checked the evidence for every single claim in the book.

After the third *New Yorker* installment ran, the book's publisher, Houghton Mifflin, received a flurry of requests for prepublication copies of the full book. Some requests came from pesticide companies and chemical industry groups. Sure enough, in August, Houghton Mifflin received a threatening letter from Velsicol Chemical Company.

Paul Brooks, Carson's editor, was alarmed. He didn't want anything to derail their publication plans. He asked a toxicologist and director of a police chemical lab to review the book alongside

Velsicol's letter, and he quizzed Carson about her sources. Satisfied, Brooks signed a response letter to Velsicol saying that Carson and the publisher were both certain about the book's accuracy. Velsicol also threatened the *New Yorker* and the National Audubon Society with lawsuits. No one buckled, and no one got sued.

Dangerous Drug

Houghton Mifflin also feared that people might lose interest in *Silent Spring* before the full book appeared in September. They needn't have worried. During the summer, a story about drug safety kept the public's attention squarely on the dangers of certain chemicals.

The drug at the center of the story was called thalidomide, developed in Germany. In Europe, Canada, Australia, Japan, and elsewhere doctors prescribed thalidomide as a sleeping pill and to ease nausea in early pregnancy. A drug company in the United States wanted to sell thalidomide too, but Dr. Frances Oldham Kelsey, a reviewer at the Food and Drug Administration, stalled its application. Kelsey, a Canadian-born pharmacologist, decided there wasn't enough evidence to show the drug was safe. She refused to approve the application, even when representatives from the drug company badgered her to sign the papers. Thalidomide was never sold in the United States.

In the countries with thalidomide for sale, more and more babies were being born with a terrible condition called phocomelia. As babies with this condition develop in the womb, their arm and

Frances Oldham Kelsey prevented the sale of thalidomide in the United States. *AP Photo*

leg bones fail to grow normally. Sometimes, the hands sprout from the shoulders and the feet from the trunk.

Doctors in Germany and Australia were beginning to suspect that the sudden increase of babies born with phocomelia might be linked to thalidomide. They were correct, and thanks to Kelsey's refusal to approve the drug, thousands of American babies escaped this awful birth defect. (The US drug company, assuming its application would be approved, gave samples of thalidomide to several hundred American doctors, who offered the samples to their patients, so some American babies were born with phocomelia.) In July 1962, Kelsey's photo and the story of her courageous stand for scientific evidence appeared in newspapers countrywide. In August, President John F. Kennedy gave her an award for distinguished service.

With people riveted to this story of heartbreak and heroism, any fears about the public losing interest in *Silent Spring's* message were unfounded. When the book hit the shelves in September, chemical misuse was front and center in people's minds. Carson recognized the link between the thalidomide story and the pesticides story. Both were examples, she told a reporter, of humans rushing to use a synthetic chemical without understanding what unintended damage it might do.

Carson's Critics

The response to the installments of *Silent Spring* in the *New Yorker* had been just a taste of what was to come. When the full book was published, it unleashed a renewed firestorm from chemical manufacturers and industry associations. The National Agricultural Chemicals Association quickly printed pamphlets refuting Carson's claims about pesticide misuse. This association insisted that Americans could never enjoy the abundant and "pure" food available in stores without the use of agricultural chemicals. One company, Monsanto, wrote a parody, or comical imitation, of the fable that opens *Silent Spring*. They called it "The Desolate Year" and described life without pesticides—and therefore *with* insects—as an economic disaster for America.

Many scientists criticized Carson too. A Harvard Medical School scientist dismissed the book as "an emotional picture," in which "Miss Carson flounders as a scientist." Another wrote a book review with the blatantly sexist title, "Silence, Miss Carson." Mainstream media also weighed in. For example, *Time* magazine accused Carson of an "emotional and inaccurate outburst" containing "oversimplifications and downright errors."

Carson's critics tried many angles to discredit her. When they had difficulty finding factual errors in the book, many of them attacked the author. They declared that Carson's scientific background—holding "just" a master's degree and not having a university job—was inadequate for her to understand and interpret science. And she wrote for the public, not for scientists. Surely, they reasoned, a credible scientist wouldn't or couldn't write in a literary style that the average reader could understand.

(left) **The cover of the first edition of *Silent Spring**. Courtesy of Houghton Mifflin Harcourt Publishing Company.*

(right) **Newspaper headlines from across the United States and Canada in 1962 and 1963.**

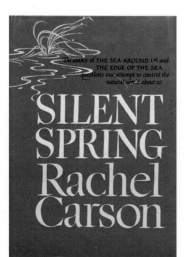

Her critics also pointed out that Carson was a woman. Women like Carson, they claimed, were "hysterical," "irrational," and "emotional," unlike male scientists. How could a woman who loved cats and nature be taken seriously when her subject was products developed and produced by the male-dominated world of science and technology?

One scientist, a British biochemist working for chemical manufacturer American Cyanamid, was particularly vocal in his outrage over *Silent Spring*. Robert White-Stevens envisioned an America without agricultural chemicals as a country plagued by hunger and disease. He gave speeches and interviews in which he accused Carson of being "a fanatic defender of the cult of the balance of nature" who used "gross distortions of the actual facts."

Though many of Carson's critics were male, not all were. Cynthia Westcott, an entomologist—a scientist who studies insects—spoke out at garden club meetings, on television, and in writing against Carson's conclusions.

The US Department of Agriculture responded to the book too, but its message was a little mixed up. At first, a representative expressed outrage and declared, "The balance of nature is a wonderful thing for people who sit back and write books." Later, however, Orville Freeman, the head of the department, ordered staff to give a more neutral message: yes, the department was aware of Miss Carson's concerns, and yes, the department shared those concerns. This message did little to reassure a public that now wondered how effectively the government safeguarded public health.

Carson's Response

Carson stuck to what she'd written in the book: She wasn't completely against the use of chemical pesticides; she was against the flagrant *misuse* of chemicals. She recognized the value of controlled "spot" spraying. She opposed widespread spraying from airplanes and trucks and the "leap now, look later" mentality of approving chemicals for use without knowing the consequences of their use. Carson advocated the old adage: "better to be safe than sorry." Decades later, scientists started using the term **precautionary principle** to mean the same thing: be cautious about using something if you don't know the effects it might have.

Carson didn't simply caution against widespread chemical pesticide use. She encouraged biological controls as an alternative response to the problem of agricultural pests. Farmers could use predator insects that prey on pest species; set out traps containing pheromones, chemicals that animals produce and release naturally; or release sterile (infertile) pest insects into the environment. She also advocated agricultural practices like crop rotation and crop diversity.

Carson remained calm during the fall of 1962 as she explained and re-explained her concerns about pesticides. She also poked fun at some of her critics. In December, in a speech to the Women's National Press Club, she mentioned a reporter who had gone out asking for opinions of *Silent Spring*. Carson quoted the reporter's comment: "No one in either county farm office who was talked to today had read the book, but all disapproved of it heartily." Carson couldn't help smiling as she told her audience this.

Carson's Admirers

Carson and *Silent Spring* drew praise as well. She received letters by the dozen. To her supporters, *Silent Spring* exposed humankind's arrogance in trying to control the natural world through science and technology. Carson had opened the public's eyes to the possibility that government agencies and large corporations put profits ahead of public interest.

Carson had also started a debate about the path society was following. Was the emphasis on buying material goods affecting people's connection with nature? Were planet Earth and its ecosystems able to sustain the uses and abuses to which humans were subjecting them? Was the focus on technological solutions to everything from medicine to space exploration to food production leading society in the wrong direction? By planting the seeds of doubt, she invited people to ponder these questions.

Carson had raised the idea of Earth stewardship—how people and society as a whole relate to our planet. We are part of the global ecosystem, not apart from it.

Many scientists supported Carson, but unlike the industry groups, they didn't have wide audiences or substantial amounts of money behind them. Hermann J. Muller, a scientist who received a Nobel Prize for his studies of gene mutations, wrote a review praising *Silent Spring*. Dr. Albert Schweitzer, a doctor, pastor, author, and humanitarian, expressed his gratitude to Carson for writing *Silent Spring* and for dedicating the book to him. Carson had drawn inspiration from Schweitzer and his guiding philosophy of "reverence for life"—meaning that all living things deserve to be respected and cared for.

Carson also found courage in praise from people like E. B. White, author of *Charlotte's Web* and a writer for the *New Yorker* magazine, who sent Carson a letter saying *Silent Spring* was "the sort [of book] that will help turn the tide." William O. Douglas, a US Supreme Court justice and champion for the environment, called *Silent Spring* "the most revolutionary book since *Uncle Tom's Cabin*." Published a century earlier, this novel by Harriet

(left) **One of the many cartoons inspired by *Silent Spring*.** *A 1963 Herblock Cartoon, © The Herb Block Foundation*

(right) **Carson standing in her study with a copy of *Silent Spring*.** *AP Photo*

"Ain't It A Beaut?"

Beecher Stowe brought the cruelty of slavery into the public spotlight. Just as *Uncle Tom's Cabin* jolted the abolitionist movement to end slavery, *Silent Spring* inspired the young environmental movement.

Roland Clement, a wildlife conservation biologist with the National Audubon Society, became a key supporter of Carson, giving speeches about her book's message. In advocating for *Silent Spring*, Clement challenged the claims of agriculture

ALBERT SCHWEITZER (1875-1965)

Born in a region of Germany that is now part of France, Albert Schweitzer studied theology and became a pastor and author. After reading about the critical need for doctors in Africa, he returned to university at age 31 and studied medicine. He specialized in tropical medicine and surgery and then traveled with his wife, Hélène Bresslau, a nurse, to Africa. They built a hospital at Lambaréné, a town now in the country of Gabon.

Not long after, World War I broke out and, being German, Schweitzer and Bresslau were taken as prisoners of war. Schweitzer returned to Lambaréné in 1924 where he spent the rest of his life as doctor, surgeon, and pastor at the hospital. He also gave organ concerts—principally Bach—in Europe to help fund the hospital, which expanded to care for more than 500 patients at a time.

Schweitzer lived by his guiding philosophy of a "reverence for life" whereby "good consists in maintaining, promoting, and enhancing life," as he wrote in one of his books *The Philosophy of Civilization*. He believed that everyone should help others. He received the 1952 Nobel Peace Prize for his humanitarian work, and with the prize money he started a facility for people with leprosy, a chronic skin infection known today as Hansen's disease.

In his later years, Schweitzer spoke out about nuclear bombs and was frustrated at being unable to persuade the world to stop making and using them.

Albert Schweitzer at his writing desk in 1955.
Trinity Mirror/Mirrorpix/Alamy Stock Photo

Draw a Cartoon

After Silent Spring appeared in 1962, newspaper and magazine cartoonists had a field day! Cartoons communicate a message about a subject or idea, and they often provoke the viewer to think more deeply about something or see a situation in a new way. A single cartoon or a short cartoon strip tends to have a narrow focus. In both drawings and words, cartoonists use tools such as:

- Exaggeration, *which is going way beyond what's really true. Saying "I got bitten by a mosquito as big as my head" is an exaggeration.*

- Irony, *which is saying or drawing something in a way that really means the opposite or shows a contrast between the situation and reality. A drawing of two people fighting their way through a blizzard with one saying to the other "What a nice day for a stroll!" shows irony.*

- Metaphor, *which is using words to suggest likeness between two things without using "like" or "as." The common saying "It's raining cats and dogs" is a metaphor.*

Try your hand at drawing a short cartoon strip about an environmental issue or situation.

You'll Need

➤ Paper, pencil, eraser, and ruler

➤ Thin black marker or pen

➤ Colored pencils or markers (optional)

1. Start by looking at the cartoons inspired by *Silent Spring* on pages 96 and 114. What do you think the cartoonists are saying or want the viewer to think about? Identify some of the tools the cartoonists used.

2. Now think about an environmental issue or situation that you want to comment on or that you want other people to think about more deeply than they otherwise might.

3. Write down a list of ideas, possible characters, words, and short sentences that you might use.

4. Think about the message you want to give to viewers and decide whether you'll draw a single-image cartoon or a cartoon strip. If you decide on a strip, aim for three image boxes: use the first box to introduce the characters and situation, the second box to build up tension, and the third box to give the punchline or ending.

5. Use a pencil and ruler (or draw freehand) to make either one large box or a series of three smaller boxes on a piece of paper. Make the boxes large enough to draw and write inside them.

6. In pencil, draw your characters and speech bubbles or other words. When everything is where you want it to be, go over the lines in black marker.

Optional: Color the cartoon if you want to. However, many cartoons are very effective when left black and white.

industry scientist Robert White-Stevens. He even debated White-Stevens on radio shows and in person.

Ups and Downs

In the months following her book's release, Carson received recognition in the form of awards—many, many awards. She received the Schweitzer Medal from the Animal Welfare Institute, the Constance Lindsay Skinner Award from the Women's National Book Association, and recognition from the National Wildlife Federation, the National Council of Women, the American Geographical Society, and the Audubon Naturalist Society.

One of the honors Carson cherished most was her induction into the American Academy of Arts and Letters. This honor society includes leading American architects, artists, composers, and writers. In 1963 when Carson was made a member, there were 50 seats, so a new member was invited to join only when an existing person left or died. Carson was one of just four female members at the time.

Throughout all the buzz, both positive and negative, Carson continued her personal struggle with deteriorating health. As her cancer spread, she was frequently in significant pain. She canceled speeches planned for some of her award acceptances and declined an invitation to travel to Sweden to give a lecture. She kept her illness secret from most people, blaming arthritis or the flu when she had to cancel events.

Throughout it all, she carried on as best she could. She even thought about her next book project. She was keen to expand the earlier article she'd published, "Help Your Child to Wonder," into a book. She also had an idea for a book about humans and nature.

Vindication

Carson declined most requests for interviews and appearances but she agreed to be interviewed for a TV news program called *CBS Reports*. The hour-long broadcast was titled "The Silent Spring of Rachel Carson."

Shortly before it was due to air in April 1963, three of the five advertising sponsors pulled out, fearing the controversy the show might generate. Nevertheless, the show went ahead with millions of Americans watching. Two interviewers spoke with Carson as well as with Robert White-Stevens and government representatives.

Carson was nervous about how she would appear on screen, since she had been ill and weak during the filming at her home the previous fall. She had worn a wig to cover her hair loss. In the end, though, Carson came across to viewers as calm, reasonable, and well-spoken. "We've heard the benefits of pesticides," she said, "but very little about the hazards . . . yet the public is being asked to accept these chemicals, is being asked to acquiesce in their use, and did not have the whole picture." Later in the show, speaking about delayed effects when children are exposed to pesticides, she said, "What is going to happen to them in adult life as a result of that exposure? We simply don't know." She said there should be laws to test pesticide chemicals for genetic effects before they are approved for sale.

By contrast, White-Stevens appeared brash and dismissive, as he sat in a laboratory wearing a lab coat. He claimed that Carson's conclusions were "completely unsupported by scientific, experimental evidence, and general practical experience in the field." Furthermore, he declared, "her suggestion that pesticides are in fact biocides destroying all life is obviously absurd." The government representatives interviewed for the show seemed out of touch and somewhat bumbling, often unable to answer questions with more than a "we don't know" or "we haven't studied that."

By the end of the broadcast, the estimated 10 to 15 million viewers, even if they hadn't already read *Silent Spring*, heard Carson's message about pesticide misuse. The program gave the final word to Carson, who said, "I think we're challenged, as mankind has never been challenged before, to prove our maturity and our mastery, not of nature but of ourselves."

Carson was pleased with the CBS show. She was also pleased when, the following month, President Kennedy's Science Advisory Committee released a long-awaited report. Early on, after the *New Yorker* installments but before *Silent Spring* was published, President Kennedy had held a news conference in which a reporter asked if the government was looking into the possible dangers of pesticides. The president replied, "Yes, and I know that they already are. I think particularly, of course, since Miss Carson's book, but they are examining the matter." In fact, his Science Advisory Committee had already been given the task of examining pesticide use. The committee later invited Carson to meet with them, which she did.

Carson—at far left, the only woman at the table—meeting with President Kennedy's Science Advisory Committee. *By permission of Rachel Carson Council, Inc.*

BRAVO FOR BIRDS

Birds mattered to Rachel Carson—she held a deep respect and love for birds and bird-watching all her life. Birds, with their colorful feathers and beautiful songs, have always appealed to people. Birds also play a vital role by providing ecosystem services—the things nature gives humans "free of charge." Scientists put ecosystem services into four categories, as shown in the chart.

Regulating	Providing	Cultural	Supporting
The services that regulate, or keep things ticking, in an ecosystem: • Cleaning water • Cleaning air • Protecting against floods • Controlling erosion • Storing carbon and regulating climate • Controlling diseases and pests • Pollinating plants	The products that ecosystems produce and humans use: • Freshwater • Food • Timber and fibers • Fuel • Energy • Biochemicals • Medicines • Genetic diversity	The intangible benefits that enrich people's lives: • Spiritual and religious significance • Recreation and ecotourism • Inspiration and tranquility • Education • Cultural heritage	The services that support all the rest of an ecosystem's functions: • Producing plant material (by photosynthesis) • Cycling nutrients • Cycling water • Making soil

Birds' services are many and varied. Examples in each category are:

Regulating: pollinating flowers, eating pest insects, carrying seeds to germinate in new places, cleaning up carcasses of dead animals

Providing: down feathers for clothes, meat for food, guano (poop!) for fertilizer

Cultural: bird-watching, spiritual meaning, subjects for art

Supporting: bringing nutrients from the ocean back to land, recycling nutrients

It can be easy to take birds for granted, or even be annoyed by bird droppings on a park bench, but we need birds. In turn, from us, birds need healthy, intact ecosystems in which to live.

Identify a Tree's Services

Rachel Carson wrote repeatedly about the web of life and how the connections between both living and nonliving things allow every living thing to exist. As living things, people are no exception. People couldn't exist without ecosystems and all their functions, or services (ecosystems, on the other hand, could exist without people).

Ecosystem services—photosynthesis, pollination, inspiration, and many more—are mind-bogglingly complex. Scientists and economists have tried placing dollar amounts on them. For example, how much would all the pollination in the world cost if people had to do it themselves? That's hard to calculate. Perhaps more valuable than pricing ecosystem services is first to recognize and appreciate them, and then to actively protect and help them.

This activity will help you see trees in a whole new light.

You'll Need

➤ The chart shown in the sidebar titled "Bravo for Birds"

➤ Photocopy of the tree diagram

➤ Pencil

➤ Colored pencils or markers

Reread Bravo for Birds (page 101) and examine the chart with the four categories of ecosystem services. Now apply the chart to trees. Which of these services do trees provide, and how? For example, trees provide water cycling services by taking water in through their roots and letting some of it out through their leaves. Fill in as many leaves on the tree diagram as you can. Add more if you need to. Color each type of service (supporting, regulating, providing, cultural) in a different color.

A TREE'S ECOSYSTEM SERVICES

STEWART UDALL (1920-2010)

Stewart Udall grew up in Arizona and became a lawyer. He was elected to Congress and then became Secretary of the Interior for nine years. During that time, he had millions of acres of land designated as national parks, wildlife refuges, and historical sites. He was involved in creating many laws to protect air, water, wilderness, and endangered species.

After he left government, Udall continued to be an advocate for wilderness, the environment, Native Americans, and an end to nuclear weapons. In 2008, he and his wife, Lee, wrote "A Message to Our Grandchildren," about the world's current environmental challenges, including oil production, global warming, energy conservation, air pollution, and wasteful consumption. They call on their grandchildren—and everyone who reads the essay—to work together "to sustain life on our small planet" using the values of "caring, sharing, and mutual efforts that reach beyond all obstacles and boundaries."

Not all government officials were hostile to Carson or her book. Stewart Udall, Secretary of the Interior under President Kennedy and a conservationist, was keenly interested in *Silent Spring*. He became the main advocate for tightening the government's policies on pesticides. One of his first moves was to open a new lab at the Patuxent Wildlife Research Center to study the effects of pesticides on wildlife. Carson couldn't attend the opening ceremony because she was having radiation treatments, but Udall paid tribute to her in his speech, saying, "A great woman has awakened the Nation by her forceful account of the dangers around us. We owe much to Rachel Carson."

In June, Carson testified to another government committee, which had been formed the day after the *CBS Reports* broadcast. The Ribicoff committee, named for Senator Abraham Ribicoff who led the work, had the job of reviewing pesticides and other environmental hazards. Carson delivered a speech to the committee and answered their questions. Two days later, she testified before another committee that was examining new government laws to limit pesticide spraying.

Now, in May 1963, the committee published its report with the simple title, "Use of Pesticides." This report criticized both the government and the agriculture industry for failing the public. CBS aired a follow-up program and asked Carson for her opinion of the report. She said she felt vindicated by it. "I am particularly pleased," she said, "by the reiteration of the fact that the public is entitled to the facts, which after all, was my reason for writing *Silent Spring*."

Final Southport Summer

Exhausted by all the attention and appearances of the previous months, Carson finally escaped to her Southport Island cottage at the end of June. It was a bittersweet summer for Carson, knowing how ill she was. Walking was more and more difficult because of pain within her bones. She still managed to spend time with her friend, Dorothy

Freeman, drinking in the beauty of her surroundings: the shore with its tide pools, the forest with its warbling birds.

In a sad ending to the summer, one of Carson's beloved cats, Moppet, died. The following morning, Carson and Dorothy went to one of their favorite spots on Southport Island and sat together watching monarch butterflies flutter through the air. The monarchs were on their southward migration, from which they would never return. Carson knew these butterflies' fate: the southward migrators spend the winter in warm places, lay eggs the following spring, and then die.

After watching the monarchs with Dorothy, Carson wrote her friend a letter saying what joy she had felt that morning. Even though the butterflies had been embarking on their final journey, it had been a "happy spectacle." She reflected that when a life comes to its end, there is nothing

Monarch butterfly.
iStock.com/XKarDoc

unhappy about it, but simply a natural closing of that life's journey. With Moppet's death on her mind, and knowing her own life was nearing its end, Carson seems to have found peace.

RACHEL'S LAST CHAPTER AND HER INFLUENCE

> "It is one of the ironies of our time that, while concentrating on the defense of our country against enemies from without, we should be so heedless of those who would destroy it from within."
> —Rachel Carson, in a letter to the *Washington Post*, April 22, 1953

Rachel Carson sat in a wheelchair, surrounded by the ancient coastal redwoods of California's Muir Woods. Though thrilled to be among these towering trees, Carson wished she could have wandered alone through the forest. But she could barely hobble with a cane, let alone walk over the spongy forest floor, thick with tree needles, mosses, and ferns.

The Pacific Ocean along the coast of California. *Rowena Rae*

Carson in 1962 when *Silent Spring* was published. *Harris and Ewing/ © Globe Photos/ZUMA Press, Inc./Alamy Stock Photo*

Later the same day, Carson's hosts took her to the Pacific Ocean. Carson had been to the Pacific only once before, on one of the trips with her government colleague, Kay Howe, to research the Conservation in Action booklets. That had been 17 years earlier. Now, Carson drank in views of the ocean, surely wishing she could explore the shoreline.

It was October 1963, and Carson had received an invitation to give the opening speech at a conference held by the Kaiser Foundation, an organization that analyzes health issues. It was a significant honor to be invited to speak at this conference, and Carson was determined not to miss it. The travel would be difficult, though, given her poor health, so her agent, Marie Rodell, offered to accompany her. Roger stayed at home in the care of Carson's research assistant.

In California, even as Carson was pushed about in a wheelchair, nobody knew how ill she really was, though some of her closer acquaintances must have had suspicions. Carson told people that her arthritis—stiffening and pain in the joints—had flared up. In reality, Carson's cancer was spreading through her body. At times, she despaired at the thought of how little time she likely had and about all the things she still wanted to write. When she managed to suppress the despair, she continued writing letters, receiving awards, and giving speeches.

Carson titled her hour-long speech to the Kaiser Foundation in San Francisco "The Pollution of the Environment." An audience of more than 1,400 people listened attentively as she explained her concerns about chemical contamination. She spoke at length about the dangers of chemicals, how they can persist in the environment, and how they can move from one region to another. She again compared the dangers of using pesticides to the dangers of nuclear testing.

In this speech, for the first time in public, Carson called herself an ecologist.

Nearing the End

Back at home, Carson found it harder and harder to hold a pen to write, because of the pain in her upper back and numbness in her right hand. Yet, she continued making plans for the future. She sent a letter (typed on her typewriter) to the president of Chatham College, which had been Pennsylvania College for Women when Carson had studied there. She accepted his invitation to be one of the college's first "Chatham visitors" the following May. The Chatham visitors program was a way to bring successful graduates of the college back to spend a few days speaking with current students.

At around this time, Carson also made plans to leave her papers—drafts of her book and article manuscripts, research notebooks, clippings, and other items related to her work—to Yale University. Yale had just opened the Beinecke Rare Book and Manuscript Library to preserve this kind of collection.

What Carson failed to plan for, though, was Roger's future. Eleven-year-old Roger had already lost his mother and great grandmother, and he was soon to lose his great-aunt and adoptive mother.

For some reason, Carson was unable to put firm plans in place for a family to take Roger in, care for him, and raise him through his adolescence. Her hope, expressed in a letter to a friend and later included in an extra note with her will, was that either Dorothy Freeman's son and his wife or Carson's friend and editor Paul Brooks and his wife would welcome Roger. But she never asked Stanley and Madeleine Freeman or Paul and Susie Brooks directly.

By mid-February 1964, Carson was uncertain that she would be able to manage the May visit she had promised to Chatham College. She wrote again to the college president canceling her attendance and saying how much she regretted doing so.

Only two months later, on April 14, 1964, at her home in Silver Spring, Maryland, Carson's heart seized. Outside her window, the bluebells nodded,

buds swelled on the trees, and birds chirped their springtime songs. Carson died shortly before the sun set. She was just 56 years old.

Rachel's Wishes

Carson had expressed only a few wishes to mark her death. One was for cremation and a simple memorial service with Reverend Duncan Howlett reading a passage from *The Edge of the Sea*. Instead, her brother, Robert, took over. He arranged a full funeral at Washington National Cathedral complete with a bronze coffin and prayers for people who died at sea.

Later, Carson's friends insisted on her cremation, and Reverend Howlett held a private service a few days after the funeral. Some of Carson's ashes were buried next to her mother's grave, and the rest were scattered by her friend Dorothy Freeman

A plaque on the rocky shore of Southport Island marks where Dorothy scattered some of Carson's ashes. The headland above this shore is where Carson and Dorothy watched monarch butterflies in late summer 1963. *Rowena Rae*

Make a Paper "Stained-Glass" Monarch Butterfly

In the last year of her life, Rachel Carson and her friend Dorothy sat together watching monarch butterflies and marveling at their beauty, fragility, and strength to fly on a long migration south.

This activity combines the fragility of colored tissue paper with the strength of black card stock to create beautiful "stained-glass" monarchs to decorate windows.

You'll Need

- Photocopy of the image shown on page 111 (enlarged to the size you want to make; larger makes it easier to cut out the interior shapes)
- Scissors
- White chalk
- Black cardstock or black construction paper
- Pencil or ballpoint pen
- One-hole punch
- Library or Internet access
- White, orange, and yellow tissue paper
- Glue stick, craft glue, or clear tape
- Thread or dental floss

1. Cut out your photocopy of the butterfly image and use white chalk to trace its outline on a piece of black cardstock.

2. Scribble chalk on the back of the photocopy of the butterfly image.

3. Lay the image face up inside the outline you drew on the black cardstock and trace over the interior black lines with a pencil or ballpoint pen to transfer the lines to the black paper. Press hard for the best effect, and if necessary, go over the faint transfer lines on the black paper with a pencil or chalk (you can also freehand draw the interior shapes onto the black paper using chalk).

4. Use scissors to cut around the outside of the butterfly and to cut out each interior shape.

5. Use the one-hole punch to punch out the circular dots around the edges of the wings and on the butterfly's head.

6. Find a color photo of a monarch butterfly in a book or on the Internet to get a sense of the colors. Cut or tear tissue paper to cover the interior shapes on the wings. Glue or tape them down on one side of the black cardstock. Use multiple layers of tissue for a deeper color on the upper wings.

7. Glue or tape a loop of thread or dental floss to hang your butterfly from the ceiling or in a window, or tape your stained-glass creation directly onto a window.

Optional: Create many butterflies and/ or other animals and tape them onto a window for passersby to enjoy on dark nights when the lights are on inside.

along the rocky shore on Southport Island. Roger went to live with Paul and Susie Brooks and their children.

Marie Rodell acted on another of Carson's wishes: she got a group of Carson's friends and colleagues together, including Shirley Briggs from her government days, to form an environmental organization. Originally called the Rachel Carson Trust for the Living Environment, it later changed its name to the Rachel Carson Council. Today, it is a national organization working on sustainability issues. Rodell also arranged for Carson's article about wonder to be published in 1965 as a book, *The Sense of Wonder*.

Carson had one more honor bestowed upon her: in 1980, President Jimmy Carter awarded her the Presidential Medal of Freedom, the highest civilian honor in the United States. Roger accepted the award for Carson, while Jimmy Carter said of her, "Always concerned, always eloquent, she created a tide of environmental consciousness that has not ebbed."

Laws to Protect the Environment

Thanks to Rachel Carson's solid science, poetic writing, and unwavering guidance, the American public began routinely asking questions and demanding change. During the decade after Carson's death, several laws were put into place: the Clean Air Act (1970), the Environmental Pesticides Control Act (1972), the Endangered Species Act (1973), and the Safe Drinking Water Act (1974). The list went on.

Back in 1963, when Carson had testified to the Ribicoff committee, she was asked about her views on pesticides and the environment. One question put to her: *Should a new government department be created to oversee environmental concerns?* Yes, said Carson. She believed it outrageous that a single government department had responsibility for both promoting the agricultural industry and regulating pesticides. This was clearly a conflict of interest.

Finally, in 1970, President Richard Nixon announced that "it has become increasingly clear that we need to know about the total environment—land, water, and air." He established the Environmental Protection Agency (EPA). In its first five years, the EPA achieved a huge amount. It set standards for air pollutants under the new Clean Air Act, and for the public water supply under the new Safe Drinking Water Act. It started working, along with Canada, to clean up the Great Lakes. It banned the use of leaded gasoline in vehicles. And it banned the use of many of the pesticides Carson had written about in *Silent Spring*, including DDT.

Ongoing Opposition

The DDT ban fueled another wave of criticism launched at Carson, and some people continue the tirade today. They accuse Carson of being responsible for the deaths of hundreds of thousands of people in countries, largely in Africa, where malaria exists. Malaria, a disease caused by a parasite and carried by mosquitoes, causes a high fever and shaking chills and can lead to severe health complications and death.

There is no denying that malaria is a terrible disease and one that needs serious attention. Yet, to blame malaria deaths on Carson is odd. The United States banned the use of DDT within its own borders. The World Health Organization (WHO) continued to use DDT in its efforts to control malaria, and it still does today.

The WHO is attempting to eradicate—get rid of—malaria from the entire world, and it uses several methods, including controlled indoor spraying of DDT and other insecticides and the use of bed nets.

In *Silent Spring*, Carson acknowledged that controlled use of pesticides had value. She wrote, "It is not my contention that chemical insecticides must never be used." Later in the book, she endorsed a modified spraying program (for agriculture) that used as many natural insect controls as possible and also used small doses of insecticides in targeted ways when needed. This type of approach—using nonchemical methods along with some targeted chemical treatments—is what the WHO advocates in its malaria control and eradication efforts.

An alarming aspect of using insecticides against disease-carrying mosquitoes is insect resistance to the chemicals. With repeated exposure and short generation times (the time for mosquitoes to produce offspring), some mosquito populations start to resist, or build up tolerance to, the chemicals. Carson wrote about malaria mosquitoes in several countries mutating in this way to survive DDT spraying. Her examples extended to other diseases, other insects, and other chemical products too.

In *Silent Spring* she wrote "no responsible person contends that insect-borne disease should be ignored." Instead, her message was that by spraying excessively, people were making two mistakes: first, they were introducing toxins with long-term and incompletely understood health effects into the environment, and second, they were ruining the chances of warding off disease-carrying insects with an effective tool—carefully applied insecticides. Carson's critics ignore the fact that she admitted the value of limited, controlled chemical use. Instead, they cite her message about the dangers of widespread spraying as fear-mongering and sounding a false alarm.

The Environmental Movement

Although *Silent Spring* seems in some ways a departure from Carson's earlier books, it was really a continuation. Carson loved the natural world, so as an ecologist she brought its intricacies to life for her readers in articles and three ocean-themed books. In her fourth book, she asked her readers to recognize nature's vulnerabilities.

The underlying theme in her books and her work as an ecologist was the idea that connections exist among all living things and their surroundings. She believed that we all have a moral obligation to protect those who can't protect themselves—children born and unborn, and the occupants of the natural world. She also believed that people will protect what they respect and love. Respect and love for the environment grow from having a sense of wonder about the natural world.

Because she called on the general public to adopt an environmental ethic, many people consider Carson the "founding mother" of the modern environmental movement. Carson wasn't the first to talk about pollution or the dangers of pesticides, but she may have been the most effective.

Even decades before *Silent Spring*, some people already had concerns about the environment and human health, especially when disasters happened. For example, in 1948, in Donora, Pennsylvania, 20 people died and more than 600 were hospitalized when a poisonous smog spewed from a steel plant. This "Big Smog" event and air quality problems in other cities brought air pollution into national headlines and led to some of the first air pollution laws.

RACHEL CARSON IN POP CULTURE

Carson and her message in *Silent Spring* entered popular culture of the 1960s in numerous cartoon strips. One showed a praying mantis asking God to bless its mother, its father, and Carson in its bedtime prayers. Another had an irate father telling his child not to use Carson as an excuse to avoid eating spinach for dinner. After Carson died, a touching cartoon showed different insects and birds gathering flowers and laying them on Carson's gravestone.

One of several PEANUTS strips, created by Charles Schulz, that referred to Rachel Carson. *PEANUTS © 1963 Peanuts Worldwide LLC. Dist. By ANDREWS MCMEEL SYNDICATION. Reprinted with permission. All rights reserved.*

Carson's ideas entered music too, such as with Joni Mitchell's hit song "Big Yellow Taxi," released in 1970. The song is about destroying nature and not realizing what we have until it's gone. It even mentions DDT with a plea to not use the pesticide and instead let birds and bees live. In 2002, the band Counting Crows recorded a version of "Big Yellow Taxi."

Over the years, *Silent Spring* has inspired more songs, instrumental pieces, a symphony, a stage play, poems, visual art displays, a postage stamp, and other tributes and responses. In 2014, a Google doodle celebrated Carson's 107th birthday.

Numerous environmental organizations also existed in the United States before *Silent Spring*. Among them were the National Audubon Society founded in 1905 to safeguard birds, the Wilderness Society founded in 1935 to protect wild places, and the Nature Conservancy founded in 1951 to preserve important ecosystems.

After *Silent Spring*, other environmental organizations formed, including the Environmental Defense Fund. This organization began informally in 1965 with a scientist on Long Island, New York, who was studying ospreys and found DDT in unhatched eggs. When the county refused to stop using DDT in its mosquito control program, the scientist and some of his colleagues joined forces with a lawyer to sue the Suffolk County Mosquito Commission on behalf of the environment. A scientist-lawyer partnership was a rare combination in the 1960s, but it worked. The group achieved a temporary order to stop DDT use, and that was enough to set them on their course, taking their lawsuit to higher and higher courts. Their relentless work, along with that of other environmental activists, ultimately led to the nationwide DDT ban that came in 1972.

Other disasters spurred on the growing environmental movement. In January 1969, an oil rig exploded off the California coast, near Santa Barbara. Within 11 days, enough crude oil had leaked from the well to coat nearly 55 miles of coastline. The Santa Barbara spill, the worst at that time in US history, devastated marine life: invertebrates, kelp beds, fish, seals, dolphins, and seabirds died in the thousands. People in the community came out in force to help the oil-coated wildlife. The president of the company that owned the oil-spewing well was puzzled, saying, "I am amazed at the publicity for the loss of a few birds." But President Richard Nixon understood the significance of the event. It was just one year later that he established the Environmental Protection Agency.

In 1969, Gaylord Nelson, a senator from Wisconsin, had struggled without much success to interest his colleagues in environmental issues. After witnessing the Santa Barbara oil spill, he decided to try a different approach that he modeled after the vocal student activists protesting the Vietnam War. He proposed the idea of holding "teach-ins" across the country as a way to raise awareness about the environment. People responded to this idea, and on April 22, 1970, about 20 million Americans held rallies, planted trees, and cleaned up litter to demonstrate their support for a healthier environment. Earth Day has grown to become a worldwide fight for a clean environment and a celebration of the Earth's fragile diversity.

Where Are We Today?

Despite progress in many areas since Carson's day, environmental issues pervade 21st-century life. We hear regularly about air pollution, tainted water supplies, chemical residues in food, forest and grassland loss, coral reef bleaching, crumbling polar ice sheets, overpopulation, contaminated wildlife, hazardous material spills, and plastic graveyards in the ocean.

Design a Poster to Raise Awareness

There are many ways to bring your ideas and concerns about the environment to the attention of other people. Rachel Carson wrote articles and books. Another way that can be effective is to design a poster to put up at school or in your community, such as at a public library or recreation center (ask for permission).

You'll Need

➤ Scrap paper for notes and planning

➤ Pencil

➤ Poster board

➤ Markers or paints and brushes

➤ Old magazines or scraps of colored paper

➤ Scissors

➤ Craft glue or glue stick

1. Think about an environmental issue that you want to highlight and about the information you want people to get from looking at your poster.

2. On scrap paper, write down some ideas for catchy phrases or titles you could use to get people's attention. Write down some ideas for actions that people could take to help or lessen the issue.

4. On scrap paper, sketch a poster design with a catchy title, an image, and brief information about the issue and the positive actions people can take.

5. On poster board, draw your design in pencil first and then add color using markers or paints and by gluing on cutouts from magazines or scraps of colored paper.

Optional: Design a small black-and-white poster and photocopy it several times before adding color. Then you can put up multiple copies so more people see your poster.

We are also witnessing more and more examples of extreme weather and other events exacerbated by Earth's currently warming climate: wickedly powerful hurricanes, more wildfires rampaging in the "off-season," and more extensive droughts, to name just a few. One difference today from the 1950s and '60s, however, is that many people are aware, many care, and many are willing to stand up and speak out for what they believe has to change.

Were Rachel Carson alive today, I think she would be saddened at the state of the environment—our environment, the only Earth we have for now and for the foreseeable future. Our globe—the tiny ball of blue and green that we see in photos taken from space—is governed by science: physics, chemistry, and biology. The laws of nature don't bow to national boundaries or political ideas. All life, humanity included, is bound by the laws of nature and the life-support systems Earth provides: the air, the water, and the soil. Sometimes referred to as Gaia, the Greek goddess of the Earth, our global ecosystem is resilient. It will adjust to the diverse assaults being launched at it, as it has done for millennia, but will the adjustments allow life as we currently know it to flourish, or even exist, on Earth?

Carson would also, I believe, be heartened by the many individuals who are working tirelessly for a healthier, more sustainable planet. Some people contribute to large environmental organizations, while others work with small groups. These include shoreline cleanup crews, community gardeners, stream keepers, tree planters, nature school teachers, citizen scientists, and the list goes on. All these people are helping not just to protect, restore, or appreciate nature but also to build ecological literacy—an understanding of how ecosystems function and how to use that knowledge to support sustainable human communities.

As well as making a difference through an organized group, we all have many options for our seemingly small daily actions. Any single action can build on another, and another, and another, accumulating over time and magnifying through a community. One family or one individual can contribute by buying less; recycling more; using reusable bags and bottles; choosing not to use pesticides; planting native plants; eating locally grown food; turning off the lights; using water sparingly; traveling by foot, bike, bus, or carpool; and demanding change from their elected officials. Even writing a poem or a story or a book can make a difference, as Carson demonstrated.

As citizens of planet Earth, you, readers, have a stake in the future and a role to play in the present. What does nature mean to you? How can you deepen your own ecological literacy and help others become more literate too? How might you draw inspiration from Carson's life and ideas?

Rachel's Influence

Carson is often remembered as the person who blew the whistle on pesticide pollution, and so she is. But her contribution to the world is so much more than *Silent Spring*. She brought an understanding of ecology to the average person by

AL GORE (1948–)

Al Gore, vice president of the United States from 1993 to 2001, has been a climate change activist for many years. He wrote a book in 2006 titled *An Inconvenient Truth: The Planetary Emergency of Global Warming and What We Can Do About It*, and he was then the subject of a documentary film with the same name. The following year he was awarded the Nobel Peace Prize for his efforts to spread the message about threats from climate change. The prize went jointly to Gore and the Intergovernmental Panel on Climate Change, or IPCC, which is an international group set up by the United Nations to examine the science of climate change.

Gore credits Rachel Carson for his involvement in environmental issues. When *Silent Spring* was reprinted in 1994, he wrote the introduction in which he described how he had read the book as a teenager and his family discussed it around the dinner table. He also revealed that a picture of Carson hangs in his office. "Her work," he wrote, "the truth she brought to light, the science and research she inspired, stand not only as powerful arguments for limiting the use of pesticides but as powerful proof of the difference that one individual can make."

A portrait of Carson painted by Minnette D. Bickel, a Pittsburgh artist, for the 25th anniversary celebration in 1987 of *Silent Spring*'s publication. *By permission of the Bickel family/Image from Chatham University Archives and Special Collections*

describing nature's many and varied connections. She showed how a single, quiet voice could reach hundreds of thousands of people not only in the United States but around the world. She showed, at a time when few women were in positions of leadership, that a woman could stand up, speak out, and be listened to. She believed that she had to make her voice heard, and she did, even though she struggled with family responsibilities and her own worsening health.

Today we face many environmental challenges. But we can surely find our way through them if we use Rachel Carson's skills: meticulous research, shrewd questioning, sheer determination, and limitless wonder at the beauty of our interconnected world.

Write a Letter to Rachel Carson

Where we would probably type an e-mail or send a text message, people used to write and send letters. Rachel Carson wrote thousands of letters throughout her life to family and friends, editors and publishers, scientists and other experts, and fans of her writing. Many she wrote by hand, and some she typed on a typewriter.

Now that you know more about Carson's ideas and opinions about nature, write her a letter about the environment today and how things have changed since she published Silent Spring.

You'll Need

➤ Paper and pen or pencil, or a computer

1. Think about what you'd like to say in your letter. You could write broadly about the environment in today's world, or you could focus on a specific topic, like DDT use since the 1960s, or bald eagle populations since the 1960s, or plastic pollution in the ocean, or one of many other topics that Carson would likely be interested in.

2. Brainstorm a list of points you could make in your letter.

3. Write the date and salutation (who the letter is to) as if you were going to mail it to Carson.

4. Then write:

   • An opening that states your reason for writing

   • A middle that explains what you want Carson to know

   • A closing to sum up your thoughts

5. Finish the letter by signing off with your name.

Optional: Choose an environmental issue that concerns you and write a letter to a politician who represents the town, state, or region where you live. Use the same format as above. (When writing with your concerns to someone like a politician, you should also ask for a response and thank the person for reading your letter.)

ACKNOWLEDGMENTS

I am deeply grateful to the many people who helped me as I researched and wrote this book about one of my heroes, Rachel Carson. My thanks go to my parents, Ann Skidmore and Angus Rae, for believing in me; to Amy O'Quinn, Elspeth Rae, Martine Street, Shari-lynn Wardrop, and Andrew Wilson for advice and encouragement at various stages of this project; to Tierra Boorman and my daughters, Genevieve Wilson and Madeleine Wilson, for their assistance in testing activities for the project and for their contagious enthusiasm; to Evonne Tang, Sean Riggs, Alyce Rae, and Cameron Stanton-Reid for putting me up and putting up with me during my "Rachel pilgrimage" in April 2018; and to my partners in West Coast Editorial Associates for hearing more than they may have wished about my "Rachel project."

I would like to thank Molly Tighe at Chatham University Archives, Pittsburgh, for access to papers and photographs on very short notice; Linda Lear for access to the collection, including photographs, she amassed while writing her 1997 Carson biography; Rose Oliveira and Benjamin Panciera for help navigating the Carson Collection at the Linda Lear Center for Special Collections and Archives at Connecticut College, New London; Anne Marie Menta at the Beinecke Rare Book and Manuscript Library at Yale University, New Haven, CT, and Caitlin Lampman at the Edmund S. Muskie Archives and Special Collections, Bates College, Lewiston, Maine, for help in finding photographs; Jeanne Cecil with the Rachel Carson Homestead Association for touring me through Carson's childhood home in Springdale, Pennsylvania; Diana Post and Clifford Hall with the Rachel Carson Landmark Alliance for welcoming me at Carson's Silver Spring, Maryland, home; Ross Feldner at the Rachel Carson Council for encouragement and help with visual materials; Roger Christie, Carson's grandnephew and adopted son for speaking with me by phone and e-mail; Martha Freeman, Dorothy Freeman's granddaughter, for permission to reproduce several photographs; Dirk, Piet, and Jane van Loon for permission to reproduce one of their grandfather's illustrations; Susan Bickel Scioli and Minnette Bickel Boesel for corresponding with me about their mother's artwork and giving permission to reproduce her painting of Carson; and Patricia DeMarco for speaking with me about her work related to and inspired by Rachel Carson.

Also very helpful in obtaining information and photographs were Diana Kenney at the Marine Biological Laboratory, Woods Hole, Massachusetts; Debbie Scanlon and Susan Witzell at Woods Hole Historical Museum; Jayne Doucette at Woods Hole Oceanographic

Institution; Jim Stimpert at Sheridan Libraries, Johns Hopkins University, Baltimore; George Perkins at the McLean County Museum of History, Bloomington, Illinois; Teri Frady at NOAA's Northeast Fisheries Science Center; Linda Weir at USGS Patuxent Wildlife Research Center; and Jeff Cramer at the Walden Woods Project.

I would especially like to thank Carolyn Combs, friend and writing partner, for commenting on drafts of the entire manuscript; Jennifer Sommer, Natalie Rompella, and Karla Moeller for commenting on parts of the manuscript; and Mark Hamilton Lytle, historian and author of a 2007 biography of Carson, for reviewing the manuscript and helping me improve it.

I also thank Lisa Reardon, who believed in this project and acquired it. And last, I give many thanks to my editor, Jerome Pohlen; my copy editor, Benjamin Krapohl; and the entire team at Chicago Review Press for shepherding the manuscript as it grew into a real book. Thank you, all!

GLOSSARY

abiotic Something that is part of the nonliving environment.

abyssal The deepest parts of the ocean.

adaptation A physical or behavioral characteristic that improves an organism's ability to survive in its environment.

algae Organisms that are similar to plants but not in the plant kingdom. Most algae photosynthesize and live in aquatic environments. Phytoplankton and seaweed are both algae.

apex predator The animal at the highest trophic level of a food chain.

benign Not harmful.

bioaccumulation The increase of a substance (typically a harmful chemical) in an organism's body during its lifetime.

biocide A substance that can harm or kill living things.

biomagnification The increase of a substance (typically a harmful chemical) at each higher trophic level in a food chain. The increase happens because animals at each level are eating food that has bioaccumulated the substance.

biome A biological community on a very large scale.

biotic Something that is part of the living environment.

carcinogen Something that causes cancer—cells growing out of control—in living things.

carnivore An organism that eats animals.

community A group of organisms that interact with each other.

consumer An organism that gets its energy from eating living or dead animals.

cycle Any pathway in nature where something circulates from one place to another, one form to another, or one stage to another.

DDT The short form of a synthetic chemical pesticide. Its full name is dichlorodiphenyltrichloroethane.

decomposer An organism that breaks down dead and dying plants and animals into basic nutrients.

ecological succession The stages an ecosystem goes through as it changes and matures over time.

ecologist A scientist who studies ecology.

ecology The science of how organisms interact with each other and with their environment.

ecosystem All the plants, animals, and abiotic characteristics that exist together in a particular place.

ecosystem services The things in nature that sustain human life and survival.

environmental movement The broad group of people working toward the common goal of protecting Earth's natural resources, ecosystems, and wildlife.

food chain The arrangement of organisms by feeding relationship. The bottom of a food chain is the lowest trophic level (producer) and the top is the highest trophic level (apex predator).

food web The combination of all the food chains in a community of organisms.

habitat The place where an organism lives within its ecosystem.

herbicide A substance that can harm or kill plants or algae.

herbivore An organism that eats plants or algae.

insecticide A substance that can harm or kill insects.

intertidal The zone of an ocean's shore between the high-tide and low-tide marks. Intertidal creatures are sometimes under water and sometimes exposed to the air.

malignant Harmful. Malignant is often used to describe a cancerous tumor.

migration The movement of an animal from one place to another, often because of changing seasons.

nearshore The zone of the sea and seabed that is close to the shore.

niche The role an organism plays in an ecosystem as a result of all the organism's interactions with abiotic and biotic things.

organism Any living thing. Animals, plants, protists, fungi, and bacteria are all organisms.

pelagic The zone of open water in the ocean or a lake.

persistent organic pollutant (POP) A harmful chemical that breaks down slowly, so it lasts for a long time in the environment. POPs also tend to be easily moved long distances in air or water, and they accumulate in organisms (bioaccumulation) and magnify up the trophic levels in food chains (biomagnification).

pesticide A substance that can harm or kill "pests," which is a broad term for any plant or animal that people want to get rid of.

photosynthesis The process that plants and algae use to convert carbon dioxide and water into sugars (for their growth) and oxygen (released to the air). The sun gives the energy needed for photosynthesis to happen.

phytoplankton Small, single-celled algae that live suspended in fresh or ocean water.

planktivore An organism that eats plankton.

plankton Any plant or animal that lives suspended in fresh or ocean water. Some can move themselves, but none can swim against a strong current.

precautionary principle The idea that humans have a duty to protect environmental and human health for people living today and for future generations.

predator An animal that catches and eats another animal.

prey An animal that is caught for food. *Prey* is also used as a verb when one animal eats another animal.

primary consumer An animal that eats producers. Primary consumers are also called herbivores, because they eat plants or algae. A primary consumer is the second layer of a food chain.

producer The lowest layer of a food chain. Plants and algae are the world's main producers through their use of photosynthesis to grow (produce) new plant material.

quaternary consumer An animal that eats tertiary consumers. A quaternary consumer is the fifth layer of a food chain.

radiation treatment A way to kill cancer cells using high doses of energy from X-rays and other sources in a controlled way.

secondary consumer An animal that eats primary consumers. A secondary consumer is the third layer of a food chain.

synthetic chemical A chemical that is made (synthesized) by humans in a science lab.

tertiary consumer An animal that eats secondary consumers. A tertiary consumer is the fourth layer of a food chain.

transpiration The loss of water from plants through their leaves, stems, and other parts.

trophic level A group of organisms that eat at the same feeding layer in a food chain. Producers are the first trophic level, and each next layer up a food chain increases the trophic level by one.

water cycle The way water circulates from place to place and changes from one form to another.

zooplankton Small animals that live suspended in fresh or ocean water.

RESOURCES TO EXPLORE

Rachel Carson's Publications

The details below are of the original publications. Each one has since been republished many times by other publishers.

Carson, Rachel. *Under the Sea-Wind: A Naturalist's Picture of Ocean Life.* New York: Simon & Schuster, 1941.

Carson, Rachel. *The Sea Around Us.* New York: Oxford University Press, 1951.

Carson, Rachel. *At the Edge of the Sea.* Boston: Houghton Mifflin, 1955.

Carson, Rachel. *Silent Spring.* Boston: Houghton Mifflin, 1962.

Carson, Rachel. *The Sense of Wonder.* New York: Harper & Row, 1965.

Books with Excerpts of Rachel Carson's Writing

Brooks, Paul. *Rachel Carson: The Writer at Work.* San Francisco: Sierra Club Books, 1989. Originally published as *The House of Life: Rachel Carson at Work.* Boston: Houghton Mifflin, 1972.

Freeman, Martha, ed. *Always, Rachel: The Letters of Rachel Carson and Dorothy Freeman, 1952–1964.* Boston: Beacon Press, 1994.

Lear, Linda, ed. *Lost Woods: The Discovered Writing of Rachel Carson.* Boston: Beacon Press, 1998.

Steingraber, Sandra, ed. *Rachel Carson: Silent Spring & Other Writings on the Environment.* New York: Library of America, 2018.

Websites and Places to Visit

The Life and Legacy of Rachel Carson

www.rachelcarson.org

This site was compiled by Linda Lear, who wrote a comprehensive biography of Rachel Carson.

Rachel Carson Council

www.rachelcarsoncouncil.org

This organization, originally named the Rachel Carson Trust for the Living Environment, was founded by Carson's friend Shirley Briggs in 1965 to continue her work. The council publishes a blog and newsletter and has a DVD copy available for rent of the CBS broadcast, "The Silent Spring of Rachel Carson."

Rachel Carson Homestead

Springdale, Pennsylvania

www.rachelcarsonhomestead.org

Rachel Carson's birthplace and childhood home is a National Historic Site that offers school visits and tours by appointment. Parts of the home have been restored to look as they did when Rachel lived there as a child.

Rachel Carson Landmark Alliance

Silver Spring, Maryland

www.rachelcarsonlandmarkalliance.org

Rachel Carson wrote much of *Silent Spring* at her Silver Spring home, which is now a National Historic Site. A corner of Carson's study has been restored to look exactly as it did in her day.

Rachel Carson's Silent Spring, A Book that Changed the World

www.environmentandsociety.org/exhibitions/silent-spring/overview

This site is a virtual exhibition created by Mark Stoll for the Environment & Society Portal hosted by the Rachel Carson Center for Environment and Society in Munich, Germany. The exhibition went live online in 2012 to commemorate the 50th anniversary of *Silent Spring*.

The Rachel Carson National Wildlife Refuge

Wells, Maine

www.fws.gov/refuge/rachel_carson/

Established in 1966 and named after Rachel Carson in 1969, this refuge stretches along about 50 miles of coastline in Maine. At the entry near Wells, visitors can walk the Carson Trail, which is a one-mile loop through pine woods and looking over tidal salt marshes.

Woods Hole Science Aquarium

Woods Hole, Massachusetts

www.nefsc.noaa.gov/aquarium

Established in 1885, this aquarium is the oldest marine aquarium in the United States and is just down the street from where Rachel Carson worked and studied during stints at the Marine Biological Laboratory. The aquarium is open to the public by donation and exhibits species found in New England waters.

Films and Videos

American Experience: Rachel Carson

www.pbs.org/wgbh/americanexperience/films/rachel-carson/

This documentary first aired in 2017. It is available through various online streaming services.

A Sense of Wonder

www.kaiulanilee.com/a-sense-of-wonder.html

Kaiulani Lee wrote and performs *A Sense of Wonder*, a one-woman play about Rachel Carson. Lee has performed the play all over the United States and abroad. It is available as a film.

The Silent Spring of Rachel Carson

CBS Reports

This documentary first aired in 1963. The Rachel Carson Council (www.rachelcarsoncouncil.org/shop) has a DVD copy available for rent.

SELECTED BIBLIOGRAPHY

Titles marked with an asterisk are especially appropriate for young readers.

Bowman, William D., Sally D. Hacker, and Michael L. Cain. *Ecology.* New York: Oxford University Press, 2017.

DeMarco, Patricia. *Pathways to Our Sustainable Future: A Global Perspective from Pittsburgh.* Pittsburgh, PA: University of Pittsburgh Press, 2017.

Dunlap, Thomas R., ed. *DDT, Silent Spring, and the Rise of Environmentalism.* Seattle: University of Washington Press, 2008.

*Lawlor, Laurie. *Rachel Carson and Her Book That Changed the World.* New York: Holiday House, 2012.

Lear, Linda. *Rachel Carson: Witness for Nature.* New York: Henry Holt, 1997.

*Lytle, Mark Hamilton. *The Gentle Subversive: Rachel Carson, Silent Spring, and the Rise of the Environmental Movement.* New York: Oxford University Press, 2007.

*MacGillivray, Alex. *Understanding Rachel Carson's Silent Spring.* New York: Rosen Publishing Group, 2011.

Matthiessen, Peter, ed. *Courage for the Earth: Writers, Scientists, and Activists Celebrate the Life and Writing of Rachel Carson.* Boston: Houghton Mifflin, 2007.

Musil, Robert K. *Rachel Carson and Her Sisters: Extraordinary Women Who Have Shaped America's Environment.* New Brunswick, NJ: Rutgers University Press, 2014.

Seager, Joni. *Carson's Silent Spring.* London: Bloomsbury, 2014.

*Sisson, Stephanie Roth. *Spring After Spring: How Rachel Carson Inspired the Environmental Movement.* New York: Roaring Brook Press, 2018.

Souder, William. *On a Farther Shore: The Life and Legacy of Rachel Carson.* New York: Broadway Books, 2012.

Sterling, Philip. *Sea and Earth: The Life of Rachel Carson.* New York: Thomas Y. Crowell, 1970.

*Wadsworth, Ginger. *Rachel Carson: Voice for the Earth.* Minneapolis, MN: Lerner Publications, 1992.

NOTES

Chapter 1: A Path to Biology

"I can remember no time": Carson, "The Real World Around Us," Columbus, Ohio, April 21, 1954, *Rachel Carson: Silent Spring & Other Writings on the Environment*, ed. Sandra Steingraber (New York: Library of America, 2018), 336.

"witchery, witchery" through *"gloriously happy"*: Carson, "My Favorite Recreation," *St. Nicholas* 49, July 1922, 999.

"rather a solitary child": Carson, "The Real World Around Us," 336.

"Rachel's like the mid-day sun": Parnassus High School Year Book, 1925, as quoted in *Rachel Carson: Witness for Nature*, Linda Lear (New York: Henry Holt, 1997), 24.

"For the mighty wind arises": Alfred Tennyson, "Locksley Hall," *The Poetical Works of Alfred Tennyson, Poet Laureate* (Boston: James R. Osgood, 1878), 60.

"That line spoke": Carson, letter to Dorothy Freeman, November 8, 1954, *Always, Rachel: The Letters of Rachel Carson and Dorothy Freeman, 1952–1964*, ed. Martha Freeman (Boston: Beacon Press, 1994), 59.

Chapter 2: Rachel Sees the Sea

"There was nothing": Carson, "Our Ever-Changing Shore," *Holiday* 24, July 1958, in *Lost Woods: The Discovered Writing of Rachel Carson*, ed. Linda Lear (Boston: Beacon Press, 1998), 118.

first experience of the sea as "glorious": Carson, letter to Dorothy Thompson, August 25, 1929, as quoted in *On a Farther Shore: The Life and Legacy of Rachel Carson*, William Souder (New York: Broadway Books, 2012), 43.

"In 1913, rock slides on": Carson, "Guarding Our Wildlife Resources," Conservation in Action 5 (Washington, DC: US Department of the Interior, 1948), 42.

"the situation in a nutshell": Carson, letter to Dorothy Thompson, August 23, 1931, as quoted in *Rachel Carson: Witness for Nature*, 72.

Chapter 3: Writing About the Ocean

"To sense this world of": Carson, "Undersea," *Atlantic Monthly*, September 1937, in *Lost Woods*, 4.

"He talked to me for": Carson, "The Real World Around Us," 337.

"seven-minute fish tales": Linda Lear, *Rachel Carson: Witness for Nature*, 78.

"My chief handed it back" and *"I had given up writing"*: Carson, "The Real World Around Us," 337.

"To Mr. Higgins, who": Philip Sterling, *Sea and Earth: The Life of Rachel Carson* (New York: Thomas Y. Crowell, 1970), 100.

"The world received the event": Carson, "The Real World Around Us," 338.

Chapter 4: Expanding Her Range

"My principal hobby is ornithology": Carson, letter to Raymond J. Brown, editor of *Outdoor Life*, October 15, 1946, *Rachel Carson: Silent Spring & Other Writings*, 318.

"very bright," "delightful," and *"more fun"*: Shirley Briggs, interview by Mark Madison, April 24, 2000, US Fish and Wildlife Service National Digital Library, https://digitalmedia.fws.gov/digital/collection/document/id/917/rec/1.

"dust the head, pumping the": F. L. Soper, W. A. Davis, F. S. Markham, and L. A. Riehl, "Typhus Fever in Italy, 1943–1945, and Its Control with Louse Powder," *American Journal of Hygiene* 45 (1947): 328.

"for his discovery of": "Paul Müller – Facts," NobelPrize.org, accessed June 4, 2019, www.nobelprize.org/prizes/medicine/1948/muller/facts/.

"We have all heard a lot": Carson, letter to Harold Lynch, July 15, 1945, *Rachel Carson: Silent Spring & Other Writings*, 315.

"method of blind flying" and *"a staccato series of"*: Carson, "The Bat Knew It First," *Collier's Weekly*, November 18, 1944, 24.

"a flying insect trap": Carson, "Ace of Nature's Aviators," manuscript, 1944, in *Lost Woods*, 25.

"The swift's idea of going": Carson, "Ace of Nature's Aviators," 26.

"a satisfactorily filled bag": "Milkweed Floss Has Important War Use," *Macon Chronicle-Herald*, July 29, 1944, 1.

"If you travel much in": Carson, "Chincoteague: A National Wildlife Refuge," Conservation in Action 1 (Washington, DC: US Department of the Interior, 1947), page preceding page 1.

Chapter 5: Under the Sea and On Top of the World

"These deep, dark waters": Carson, *The Sea Around Us* (New York: New American Library, 1961), 48.

"Out of the clear green water": Carson, *Under the Sea-Wind* (New York: Oxford University Press, 1952), 129.

"fierce and ravening as a pack of wolves": Carson, *Under the Sea-Wind*, 130.

"I assume from the author's" and *"I thought you would be"*: Carson, "The Real World Around Us," 335.

"As they roll majestically": Carson, jacket notes for *La Mer*, composed by Claude Debussy, RCA Victor Recording, 1951. Reprinted in *Lost Woods*, 87.

Chapter 6: The Wonder of Nature

"Those who contemplate the beauty": Carson, *The Sense of Wonder* (New York: Harper & Row, 1965), 88.

"roasted the script": Carson, letter to Dorothy Freeman, September 28, 1953, *Always, Rachel*, 6.

"done it again": Lear, *Rachel Carson: Witness for Nature*, 262.

"To Dorothy and Stanley Freeman": Carson, *The Edge of the Sea* (New York: The New American Library, 1955).

"yet in a constantly renewing": Carson, script for "Something About the Sky," *Omnibus*, aired March 11, 1956. Reprinted in *Lost Woods*, 181.

"We are going to pretend": Carson, "Something About the Sky," 177.

"If I had influence with": Carson, *The Sense of Wonder* (New York: Harper & Row, 1965), 42.

Chapter 7: Everything Is Connected

"Wildlife . . . is dwindling": Carson, "Fight for Wildlife Pushes Ahead," *Richmond Times-Dispatch Sunday Magazine*, March 20, 1938. Reprinted in *Lost Woods*, 15.

"No one yet knows": Carson, *Silent Spring* (Boston: Mariner Books, 2002), 23.

"Though the sedge is withered": John Keats, "La Belle Dame Sans Merci," *The Complete Poetical Works of Keats* (Boston: Houghton Mifflin, 1899), 139.

"a brilliant achievement": Carson, letter to Dorothy Freeman, January 23, 1962, *Always, Rachel*, 394.

Chapter 8: When Birds Can't Sing

"No witchcraft, no enemy action": Carson, *Silent Spring*, 30.

"an emotional picture": Frederick J. Stare, "Some Comments on Silent Spring," *Nutrition Reviews*, January 1, 1963, 1.

"Silence, Miss Carson": William J. Darby, "Silence, Miss Carson," *Chemical & Engineering News*, October 1, 1962, 60.

"emotional and inaccurate outburst": "Pesticides: The Price for Progress," *Time*, September 28, 1962, 47.

"a fanatic defender of the cult": Robert White-Stevens, interview by Eric Sevareid, "The Silent Spring of Rachel Carson," *CBS Reports*, April 3, 1963.

"The balance of nature is": Lear, *Rachel Carson: Witness for Nature*, 413.

"No one in either county": Carson, speech to the Women's National Press Club, Washington, DC, December 5, 1962, in *Rachel Carson: Silent Spring & Other Writings*, 431.

"the sort [of book] that will": Lear, *Rachel Carson: Witness for Nature*, 421.

"the most revolutionary book": Lear, *Rachel Carson: Witness for Nature*, 419.

"Good consists in maintaining": Albert Schweitzer, *The Philosophy of Civilization, I: The Decay and Restoration of Civilization*, trans. C. T. Campion (New York: Macmillan, 1949), 79.

"We've heard the benefits" and *"What is going to happen"*: Carson, "Silent Spring of Rachel Carson."

"completely unsupported by scientific" and *"her suggestion that pesticides"*: Robert White-Stevens, "Silent Spring of Rachel Carson."

"I think we're challenged": Carson, "The Silent Spring of Rachel Carson."

"Yes, and I know that": John F. Kennedy, "The President's News Conference," August 29, 1962, The American Presidency Project (website), Gerhard Peters and John T. Woolley, accessed June 5, 2019, https://www.presidency.ucsb.edu/documents/the-presidents-news-conference-187.

"to sustain life on our": Stewart Udall and Lee Udall, "A Message to Our Grandchildren," *High Country News*, March 31, 2008.

"I am particularly pleased": Lear, *Rachel Carson: Witness for Nature*, 452.

"A great woman has awakened": Stewart Udall, US Department of the Interior press release, April 25, 1963, as quoted in *On a Farther Shore: The Life and Legacy of Rachel Carson*, William Souder (New York: Broadway Books, 2012), 380.

"happy spectacle": Carson, letter to Dorothy Freeman, September 10, 1963, *Always, Rachel*, 468.

Chapter 9: Rachel's Last Chapter and Her Influence

"It is one of the ironies": Carson, "Mr. Day's Dismissal," letter to the *Washington Post*, April 22, 1953, *Rachel Carson: Silent Spring & Other Writings*, 325.

"Always concerned, always eloquent": Jimmy Carter, "Presidential Medal of Freedom Remarks at the Presentation Ceremony," June 9, 1980, The American Presidency Project (website), Gerhard Peters and John T. Woolley, accessed June 5, 2019, https://www.presidency.ucsb.edu/documents/presidential-medal-freedom-remarks-the-presentation-ceremony.

"it has become increasingly clear": Richard Nixon, "Reorganization Plan No. 3 of 1970," July 9, 1970, EPA's Web Archive, US Environmental Protection Agency, accessed June 5, 2019, archive.epa.gov/epa/aboutepa/reorganization-plan-no-3-1970.html.

"It is not my contention": Carson, *Silent Spring*, 12.

"no responsible person contends": Carson, *Silent Spring*, 266.

"I am amazed at the publicity": Keith C. Clarke and Jeffrey J. Hemphill, "The Santa Barbara Oil Spill: A Retrospective," in *Yearbook of the Association of Pacific Coast Geographers* 64, ed. Darrick Danta (University of Hawai'i Press, 2002): 157–162.

"Her work, the truth she brought": Al Gore, introduction to *Silent Spring*, Rachel Carson (New York: Clarion Books, 1994), xxvi.

INDEX